THE GREGORY ANTHOLOGY
1987–1990

The Gregory Anthology 1987–1990

edited by
Alan Brownjohn and K.W. Gransden

Hutchinson
London Sydney Auckland Johannesburg

This edition first published in 1990 by
Hutchinson

Century Hutchinson Ltd, Random Century House,
20 Vauxhall Bridge Road, London SW1V 2SA

Century Hutchinson Australia (Pty) Limited,
20 Alfred Street, Milsons Point, Sydney, NSW2061, Australia

Century Hutchinson New Zealand Limited,
PO Box 40–086, Glenfield, Auckland 10, New Zealand

Century Hutchinson South Africa (Pty) Ltd
PO Box 337, Bergvlei, 2012 South Africa

British Library Cataloguing in Publication Data

The gregory anthology.
  1. Poetry in English – Anthologies
  I. Brownjohn, Alan, *1931-* II. Gransden, K.W. (Karl Watts), *1925-*

  ISBN 0-09-174493-8

Set in Times by ⚑ Tek Art Ltd
Printed and bound in Great Britain by Cox and Wyman Ltd, Reading

Contents

JOHN WELLS

Introduction

This anthology, the fifth of its kind, comprises selections from the manuscript submissions of each of the twenty-two poets given 'a Gregory' in the years 1987–1990. It appears in the thirtieth year of the Eric Gregory Award, which has become one of the most generous and celebrated of the annual literary prizes; so it seems both timely and appropriate to say something about its founder and his intentions.

Dr E.C. Gregory was a publisher and printer (Percy Lund Humphries and Co., of Bradford and London) who had a profound patron's interest in furthering the arts. In the early 1950s he established Gregory Fellowships at the University of Leeds for poets and artists who needed time and financial support to practise their art; and he hoped that the Fellows would make their own kind of contribution to the university community. At his death in 1959, he left the residue of his Estate to the Society of Authors to be administered as a Trust Fund for the encouragement and assistance of poets under the age of thirty.

The first award was made in 1960. Then, and in every year since, the panel of Gregory judges needed to choose between a large number of applicants who submitted substantial bodies of work; currently there are about 130 manuscript entries every year. Dr Gregory wanted to foster ability and promise, but it was also stipulated that the circumstances of the poets should be carefully considered.

When the poets on a short-list of perhaps half-a-dozen are interviewed, both these factors are taken into account. This procedure has produced choices with which past Gregory panels are entitled to be very pleased: among the award-winning poets have been Geoffrey Hill (1961), Michael

Longley (1965), Seamus Heaney (1966), Douglas Dunn (1968), John Mole (1970), Paul Muldoon (1972), Andrew Motion (1976), Carol Ann Duffy (1984) and many other well-known names.

The judges for the years represented here, forming a panel of seven which operates a principle of rotating membership, were Dannie Abse, Alan Brownjohn, Elaine Feinstein, John Fuller, K.W. Gransden, Peter Porter, Christopher Reid, Anne Stevenson, Anthony Thwaite and Margaret Willy. At judges' meetings there is a stimulating sense that the panel (as one of its recent members put it) is 'spotting present talent and choosing for the future'. This present anthology, covering as it does four years instead of the usual two, offers readers a particularly rich opportunity to do just that.

Alan Brownjohn
K.W. Gransden

Steve Anthony

TRADING TOOLS
for my father

Hammered in and out of me, early on,
the need to be like him, and earn
my living by an honest trade.

'He's good with his hands,' was only true
of him, not me. A papier-mâché monster,
or later, in woodwork, a treacherous footstool,
were my closest approaches to craft.

He was the one for models, pinching
Plasticine into elephants or giraffes.
And once, exploring his sanctuary,
I saw a white man's head, which stared

at me through blank, deathly eyes. Crying
for civilization to come to my rescue,
she soothed me with sense. Just a sculpture.

It recalls now, how he painted our ancestry:
singers, dancers, artists; we had fallen
from our birthright, like the d'Urbervilles.

Money made him re-upholster chairs –
his mouth full of tacks, like fillings,
as he spoke or brought the hammer to his lips –
money, and the wartime education
he'd escaped, and could not return to.

1

Here we cross, two plotted characters: I study
my bookish ignorance, his life's work.
We are caught inside a text we cannot see.

But I have it by heart, I need no score
to fill the unsung silences with music

he might hear; proving our kinship
in diversity, handling different tools
to remake ourselves, like actors.

As we grow apart and together, permit me
to peer into our privacies, for love.

EARTHSWIMMER

scooping soil as water:
100 metres snout-and-claw stroke.

Worms sucked up like seaweed,
grubs gobbled – plankton
there for the picking. Then diving
deeper to sleep it off, safe

in earthpool. From the shallows,
the sound of forepaws paddling
under the surface, where footfalls
startle strata like depth-charges.

Braille-blind, feeling a way through
dark language: dank, gravesmell
rising, as a periscope for spring,
to sniff neat air.

ALIVE AND INTERESTED

I am something like that;
Only I am not dead,
Still breathing and interested
In the house that is not dark.
           Edward Thomas

I had hoped for a Blakean rebirth,
A planetary shift of emphasis;
A light revealing all in its true worth,
Blinding me from blindness gladly missed;

A rediscovery of that knowing innocence
With which children mould walls of sand,
Soon seeing they must suffer from experience
Of tide effacing work that's done by hand.

But young bones break and mend, becoming tall
Enough to stand blows and remain –
Like bricks that build up to a windowed wall,
Admitting sun and stones hurled through the pane.

So now it is your voice which speaks to me
From two world wars away, still understood:
If, like you, I cannot quite be free,
At least I am alive and interested.

SWANSONG

Oakleaves spatter the grass:
gauntlets flung for a duel
between seasoned opponents.

The beech is dripping blood,
but rallies its strength
for a last display; its leaves

are dull as scabs on the surface,
yet shot with capillaried light
within, like fingers over a lamp.

Geraniums flirt from balconies
with foppish dahlias, deferring
their windblown fate.

Plums burst; apples grow proud
as prima donnas; and everywhere,
everything strives to excel

in its annual finale.
This is autumn's aria:
a draught, heady with death.

HER FINAL PERFORMANCE

Like snow upon the desert's dusty face,
Lighting a little hour or two – is gone.
                                    Omar Khayyam

When we arrive the windows are sealed.
A neighbour unlocks this vault,
and we climb down, anxious as parents
outside a casualty ward, afraid
we might not find her alive. At last

we confront the bedroom door: it shudders
open, into a chamber enclosing her effigy,
her few possessions wrested from living.
She stirs, blinks wide, her hair shocked
white as these unwashed net curtains.

***

Beyond her dressing-room, the stage
is decked with roses, teacups, cake:
all the props for a presentation.

She enters in apron and slippers,
with cigarette cocked, on cue
for our chorus of *Happy Birthday*.

Blowing out candles, she is a child;
cutting the cake, a bride again:
with time in store to retell now,

as it nearly was, in photographs.
Cast in furs or swimsuit, she smiles
at herself half a century later,

surviving her critics: age, the deaths
of loved ones. 'You miss them,' she says,
closing the album and conversation.

***

Shadows lengthen like the silences
severing our speech. We must go
back to our selfish lives, but first
are made to accept her gifts.
One is a book of poems, pages

mottled as the hands that marked
their lines of epitaph, shattering
our youthful mirage. Beyond words
now, we can only kiss her in turn,
and leave her once more entombed.

Maura Dooley

MISSILES OVER BUXTON

On the ridge road down through windy Derbyshire,
Watching trees shake themselves in a mild autumn
I see a devil's fork rise into sleepy cloud.

Lights in the sky: a gently arcing evil.
When I ask, 'What is it?' my heart is plunging
Into downy silence. Surely it must be a dream?

This year we are trawling Halley's comet,
Other times I've fished for falling stars and
Hoped I'd never catch this nameless terror.

In a second's hour of silence, before your safe reply,
I see my mother's face, Aunty Kitty's neat back garden,
My father's hair, your eyes, your hands.

A moment's strangeness tricked us: the half light,
The greenness, no other car on this long damp road,
Under the thinning trees, the clouds, the radio masts.

Later in Buxton Opera House, I tilt borrowed glasses
At the cherubs. They crease rosy cheeks, flash gilded wings,
Cross dimpled thighs, wreathing the stage with joy.

Outside, above the hills of windy Derbyshire,
Stars dance between those radio masts, a comet nears,
The air waves glitter with important messages.

CORNWALL 1948

In Charlestown Bay the sea lapped in like milk,
Creamy with china clay. The beach a still small shell
At the end of a dusty street, curled up in the sun.

You crossed the country on your fiery Norton,
She was a crab on your back and her flowery dress flew,
All day long summer beat your hearts together.

And in the deepest bowl she cracked two eggs
First of the new day's, fresh laid: war was over;
This sponge was lighter than any they had known.

In Truro shopkeepers shook out clean blinds like flags,
You chose ripe plums under their stripey shield and
Later buried the dull stones in warm sand.

But knowing they'd never grow green you climbed
To the tiny church's salty heights, your lips parched,
Your eyes aching, looking so hard for Lyonesse.

THE WOMEN OF MUMBLES HEAD*

The moon is sixpence,
A pillar of salt or
A shoal of herring.
But on such a night,
Wild as the wet wind,
Larger than life,
She casts a long line
Over the slippery sea.
And the women of Mumbles Head
Are one, a long line,
Over the slippery sea.
Wet clothes clog them,
Heavy ropes tire them,
But the women of Mumbles Head
Are one, a long line,
Over the slippery sea.
And under white beams
Their strong arms glisten,
Like silver, like salt,
Like a shoal of herring,
Under the slippery sea.
And they haul
For their dear ones,
And they call
For their dear ones,
Casting a long line
Over the slippery sea.
But the mounting waves
Draw from them,
The mountain waves
Draw from them,

The bodies of their dear ones,
O, the bodies of their dear ones,
Drawn under the slippery sea.
In a chain of shawls
They hook one in,
Fish-wet, moonlit,
They've plucked him back
From under the slippery sea.
For the moon is sixpence,
A pillar of salt or
A shoal of herring,
And the women of Mumbles Head
Are one, a long line
Over the slippery sea.

*The women rescued a lifeboatman by making a rope of their knotted
shawls, after the Mumbles lifeboat was lost in a storm in 1883.

SECOND GENERATION

'There's just no fuchsia in it,' my Dad would joke,
But my dreams are hedged with red and purple,
Seal-lined, damp under blue mountains, caught like a burr
On this country's old coat that I try to shrug around me.

It's one long past of never having a future and
Taking the slow boat to a better land,
Needing to fill stomachs with something more than prayer,
Shedding a language, watching the shore grow small.

We want the tongue they took such care to lose,
To feel its shuffling sadness in our mouths,
We want to feel this greenness like a skin,
To scratch it when it itches, watch it heal.

Wearing the Claddagh ring, hoping its two hands
Would hold, not tear, this tiny heart,
Could I slip in there to watch the sea shift
Or cut some warmth out of a peaty soil?

No Siege of Ennis in the Irish Club,
No convent childhood, shamrock through the post,
Can net us back across that narrow passage
Nor make this town a place we can call home.

VISITING

Watching the soapy swill trickle away,
Cloudy in soft water, a scum on hard,
Glittering over Armitage Shanks
Or Twyford's vitreous enamel.
And from the window a mountain,
A back wall, a square of blue sky somewhere,
Through net, through frosted glass,
Through an open window. Visiting.

Trying to imagine how it would be
To live out this life, I have
Loitered by estate agents' windows
And done up that old shack in spare weekends.
But in these distant friendly bathrooms,
Though I use your soap and borrow towels,
My toothbrush rests uneasy on the shelf.

Stephen Knight

THE AWKWARD AGE

His diary is packed with non-events –
Like March the first *I got up late* and March the third
My teeth are visibly longer, both my cheeks are furred.
When the eristic charm of female scents

Leads me on, I follow it till I'm heard.
He sniffs at the Rive Gauche in my room! – If I say
Anything at all to him, he either turns away
  Or stares at me with his big eyes. He purred

Like a car in his bedroom yesterday,
Watching television with the curtains drawn. *Hair*
Sprouts like hair but quicker. Skin thickens. Claws grow out
where
  Nails were bitten down – I'm quoting from May

The fourth. He is obsessed with girls: their hair,
Their hands, the colour of their eyes . . . *T. said hullo*
Again today – she even smiled! But she wouldn't go
  To the cinema with me. C'est la guerre!

He's full of Wordsworth's poetry: like snow,
Books gather at the foot of his bed. When I tell
Him to tidy his things away, he says he's unwell
  Or working – he walks to the beach below

The golf links almost every night! The smell
Of salt lingers on his trousers and his best tweed
Jacket for days. There's no need to go, I say, no need.

14

(We can't seem to bring him out of his shell.)

I love, he says on June the tenth, *to feed*
The seagulls till they're nice & fat. They don't take fright
If I look them in the eye. Should I be less polite
  & try this trick with girls? Would I succeed?

Frosty looks are bad enough, but he might
Stop walking with a stoop for me. *Why can't I be*
(He writes on June the twenty-third) *smooth-skinned & sexy?*
  We get no peace. He shaves three times a night.

IN CASE OF MONSTERS

On the way to bed a) Take the staircase
Slowly. Note how many steps. Never race
To the landing or try to chase
Shadows into corners.

b) Place books and comics under your bed –
The Bible is still a safe bet c) Spread
Some knives nine inches from your head.
Polish them first. Ask Dad

Nicely and he may sharpen them for you.
d) Always *jump* into bed: monsters queue
Behind the valance until dew
Curdles on the garden.

e) Face the door before you go to sleep.
Remain like that all night. Use string to keep
Yourself in place then f) Count sheep
To save strain on the knots.

NB Always have your bed well away
From windows and let the room breathe all day
But never, never when the grey
Evenings give way to night.

g) Watch the pattern in your curtains change
To things at sunset altogether strange.
In the silence, they rearrange
Their disenfranchised smiles.

When you hear your heartbeat on the pillow
h) Count every thump, and if you don't know
Now the number of steps to go
Before your blood ascends

i) Check the knives.

AGAINST TERRARIUMS

By nine o'clock my mother is curled asleep
On a chair surrounded by greenery.
She'll have finished a cup of poisonous tea
Doctored, I suspect, with tablets and cheap

Cream sherry. This frosty, domestic tableau
Is supplemented by my father – he
Rinses the cup as her folded arms slowly
Unfold. They shift (just shift) towards that glow,

Fluorescence, at the foot of our kitchen door
Like shoots . . . Talking to her Busy Lizzie,
A confidante since 1973,
She affects her tone of voice. I ignore

Her grandiosity on the telephone;
She treats me like a rose, though I'm nearly
Twenty-two. 'Are you short of clothing? Tell me,'
She demands, then, 'Do you still sleep alone?'

THE GIFT

My parcel was delivered to the college
Thoroughly packaged, like an only child . . .
I tear my father's beautifully written note
(Please acknowledge receipt, Love Mam & Dad)
Then fold the wrapping for possible re-use.
A breeze laps the posters crusting the wall;
Like lily pads, they compete to face the light.

I bump into Philip inside the Lodge.
He asks to see the gift – another four-sleeved
Pullover! Raising it shoulder-high, he
Teases me about the additional arms
Till I make my excuses and leave him
At the pigeonholes to scurry to my room.

I lay the jumper on my coverlet
And step back to survey the lively design –
Summery shades of green and blue in bars
A centimetre wide around the middle;
And seagulls, too. Trying it on before
My full-length mirror, I turn in circles like
A weather vane. The sleeves rotate with me!

Dizzier than Lewis Carroll's Alice, I
Finish instead an essay due at six . . .
My sides itch as I write. Just below the ribs,
Above my pelvis, carpal bones, knuckles,
And ten fingernails push through the flesh like roots.
Should I telephone home, or should I wait?

SHC

Since you left, my top shelf is thick with aerosols
(Hair lacquer, dry shampoo) and a miniature
Tub of drugs. The evening soaks into my curtains.
Waiting for your call, I stay indoors all day
   To spend more time with mirrors and water.

My hair is expiring on my head. The last time
I caught my reflection in your scurrilous,
Perfect teeth I was using a comb *and* a brush!
The yucca you gave me is sending up shafts
   Of green that flicker thickly on my sill.

My tins, apparently, are quite combustible.
The hairsprays fizz and sigh; their phoney perfumes
Hang in the hallway, entering my lungs as glue.
1. If I ever pass you in town, I have
   My photograph of us: undiminished,

Your black hair is lapping your forehead and shoulders –
Unquenchable, and deeper than I recall.
My fingers could drown. 2. When I do go out, I
Walk along the seafront, moving in and out
   Of the beach huts and the tennis courts like sand.

3. I blame the lacquer for my stomach churning
As I wait for you to call. 4. My palms are
Cobwebbed and sweaty. 5. I fret as I approach
My twenty-fifth birthday . . . These numbered details
   Dampen my letters to you like drizzle;

Is that why you never telephone? although I
Write *I love you still*? I could burst into flames
Given the proper reasons. Above me, gathered
Like surf, my tins and tub agree. I rejoice
    In their promise to stiffen, clean and dope.

Peter McDonald

SILENT NIGHT

St Aubin's Bay, Jersey, 1946

It's summer now, or nearly. Out at the back door, my sister
shows the children how to feed the birds, scattering pieces
of crust into the garden: some sparrows, a couple of starlings
come down and squabble, fly off at the children's applause.
In the bathroom, I'm weighing myself – another stone –
      smiling,
hearing my name called, catching rich smells from the
      kitchen.

Those weeks when they came to take my story for the
      wireless
I had to be coaxed at first; they seemed to be after
more than names, or names and facts; they wanted to know
how it felt then, and sounded, what it tasted and smelt like,
though really it was like nothing, nothing before or since,
which I told them, and they understood, they said. But even
      so.

But even so, as they added, there was a story to be told,
and I was the man to tell it. First, there were questions
and answers, *What did you see then? And what were you*
      thinking?
But after a while, the story came out of its own accord
and there were the details they wanted, the smells and the
      sounds,
memories that had never made sense, for once locking into
      each other.

22

The first place they took you. At Wilhelmshaven that winter,
when each afternoon would preserve the frost of that
        morning
and at night there was only hail to cut into the tracks
of their lights, they bundled me with a couple of dozen
newcomers into one of the big huts, my feet touching
the ground for the first time since the court martial in Jersey.

How many in the hut? There were nearly a thousand,
crammed three to a bed, head to toe in the bunks and
        making
barely a sound. Near enough a thousand men. Packed
that tightly, you soon learn how to sleep without moving,
and you learn not to speak, you learn to lie still and say
        nothing
when there are guards on hand to force up the value of
        silence.

It was part of Neue Gamme, and I'd been brought over
from France with the others – Jean de Frotté, Bernard
Depuy, just to give two names as examples, the first one
tall, wispy-haired and delicate, the son of a marquis,
then Bernard with his square head screwed right on his
        shoulders,
though they have their own stories, parts of mine and still
        different.

We had three things to think about: food, sleep and work,
but no real need to think, for they were all taken care of,
especially the last. Once a day, there was thin turnip soup
and a crust of bread, a few hours of motionless sleep,
then the hard tramp through frost out to the Kriegsmarine
Arsenal, a day's work hearing the punch and clang of the
        riveters,

avoiding the welders' blue clouds of sparks; sweat and iron;
then our convicts' shuffle back to the camp in the dark,
their searchlights tailing us and filling in the distance
back to the gates, our hut with its three hundred bunks.
I mentioned guards: there were guards of course, but worse
were the Chiefs, one to each hut. Ours was called Omar.

You might ask me to describe, explain him, but I can do
      neither,
I can tell you his build, his features, even mimic his voice,
but that would add up to nothing, or nothing more really
than just a man in a story, maybe a bit of a monster,
a dead man anyhow. Yes, by now he'll be safely dead.
It might be easier, really, for you to explain him.

Omar, then, it turns out, had once, like most of the others,
been a prisoner himself, a young man when they caught him
in '33, they said, some kind of radical journalist.
He'd been through worse than this in his time, worse
      beatings,
work, cold and the rest, and he was in for a lifetime.
Drop by drop, I suppose, the fight just bled out of him.

So by the time the camps all got busy they made him an
      offer,
to serve his time as an *Alteste* in places like Neue Gamme
with at least enough freedom there to do as he pleased
and get on with the job. Yes, the words apply, brutal, a
      sadist
just like the others, inhuman. And yes, there are stories.
I try to remember my friend Bernard's straight talking,

'Don't judge this place, this bloody madhouse, by the
      standards
of what we've all left behind: it has a code of its own,

a lunatic code, I know, but you just have to learn it.
Lie still and say nothing.' So what is there for me to say now
about Omar? Just the truth, just what I remember?
But I couldn't call it the truth then, and now that I tell you

the stories, does that make them all true? Does it make them
happen, happen properly for the first time? It's harder,
watching the sea relax under the first mild summer evening
and waiting for dinner, too, harder to force those things
to happen again, and here, than just to keep silent. And lie?
Here by the bay, there's really no such thing as silence,

what with the waves breaking all night, and the seabirds
carrying on as usual each day. On the wireless, they tell me,
you can do wonders, but the one thing you can't get away
                with
is silence, the fretful noise of empty spaces, the worrying
gaps bare of music or talk, with just the sound of the
                atmosphere
coming into your very own room. I can give you two stories

concerning Omar, though whether or not they go well
                together
I myself couldn't say. The first happened only a few weeks
after we arrived at the camp: an Alsatian boy of sixteen
had been caught making off with some scraps of food from
                the plates
of patients dying in the infirmary (though that was hardly a
                hospital
as you'd understand the word – a dirty, overcrowded tin hut).

He came up before Omar, of course, who glared and let his
                face buckle
in on itself with disgust, then brought out the worst of his
                voices,

the fabulously wicked giant, to himself above all.
'You, boy,' he thundered down, 'you have committed
the one unforgivable crime; you have gone out and stolen
not only from your comrades, but from your sick comrades.

I'll tell you exactly how you can expect to be punished:
you're going to be made to learn the real meaning of hunger,
but you'll dread the food in your mouth; and when you leave
      us
you'll be raving mad, child, gibbering away somewhere to
      die.'
He was perfect. Large as life and much more monstrous than
      any
caricature. We kept quiet; the boy cringed and was carried
      away.

The usual stamping, shouting and beating. Then the wet
      blankets
to sleep in as well, for nights on end. They starved him,
then force-fed him salted food, served up on a scalding
hot spoon, day after day, all the while refusing him water.
By the time they finally lost interest, he looked like a
      skeleton;
unable to eat for the burns on his mouth, his scarred lips and
      tongue,

he would scream at the sight of a spoon. He died soon, of
      course,
raving mad, as Omar had promised. Now I can barely
      imagine
such things happening at all, but they did, and do still
in theory, in places far removed from this island,
the standard horrors, common knowledge now more than
      ever,

more than just hearsay these days: newsreels, words on the
     air.

And then of course there's that second *vignette*: the very
     same Omar –
who was, needless to say, cultured, had once been a classical
musician, to add to his attributes, always a lover of Mozart –
in the Christmas of '44, Omar's treat for the prisoners.
Imagine one of the huts that's been specially cleared for the
     purpose,
with benches there now and a stage, the audience all silent

(though you'd hardly mistake their silence for hushed
     expectation,
it being plainly enough the schooled silence of fear)
and then you make out a Christmas tree just to the right of
     the stage,
a piano likewise, the feeling of something about to begin.
Then suddenly Omar and the six other *Altesten*
troop on like schoolboys, heavy, bloated, all with straight
     faces.

For this is the carol service, and these fat men are the
     carollers.
Listen, and you'll pick up easily Omar's gentle booming
among all the voices here. In fact I myself was arrested
for 'communal listening'; I suppose it's just what I'm good at.
But no actor alive could reproduce the sound of this memory,
that music in the hungry, cold air, *Stille nacht, Heilige nacht.*

On clear evenings, I watch those rocks on the near side of
     the bay,
a circle of broken teeth, finally blotted out by the tide.
I hear the seabirds roosting for miles along the whole
     coastline,

and then there's just the sea noise and the sound of the
        wireless
with its bad and good news, the music of Victor Sylvester,
the Epilogue, the King, the whisper and fizz of the
        atmosphere.

Some nights I think I see the dead and living stand in a
        circle,
naked but for their memories, and in full view of each other,
immobile as those rocks crumbling gradually into the bay,
as though they were trying to speak, or cry, or scream in the
        silence,
to hear each other and understand; but the dead weight of
        stone
holds us all down, makes us stand still and say nothing.

So now that they call me to dinner, and I laugh with the
        children
over this or that story, I know I'll catch myself thinking,
not of the past exactly, but more of that programme,
my voice and the voices of actors, and somewhere among
        them
Jean and Bernard alive, Omar's Christmas carol; the last
winter of a bad war; a boy with a horror of spoons.

Jill Maughan

HILL END

If our coming was a spring, then our going is well caught
in this biting season, though our small embrace
meets poorly with the features of this vast, moorland face,
with its voice as penetrating as a raging, windy day,

and its hilltop snow like the white hair on a wise man's head.
But the stone wall lines that cut like secateurs
tell of a kind of inextractable pain, walking here with you,
crossing these icy patches, and even in our knowing

we have a hundred miles to go and a lifetime, none of this
compares to what is wrought in the iron stare of this place.
Our years are hardly a graze on this skin and our
energy almost a trespass on this living silence.

But our purpose as much as our past is breathing
on the haunting road of this familiar route,
and is breathing too, in the house at the end of the hill,
which is 'sold' and to which we will not return.

VASE

Sometimes I think I will be here forever,
always like this, permanent and sure of tomorrow,
and the house too, unmovable and resilient.
The roses that flare up the stone walls
will return each summer, and sometimes
I can barely believe this will change.

But yesterday, having caught a glance
of someone else's despair,
I lay awake and fear blew in from
the open window, and I turned and tossed
but saw life sweep away in the shadows
that sailed across the stone walls,

and there I saw myself weak at the knees,
shorebound and alone, with many important words
left unsaid, and a mass of untied threads
clutched like promises,
and loves that wailed down the years,
all broken and fragmented pieces of a vase
I had once thought could not shatter.

GHOST OF LOVE

Go home, ghost of love and sleep,
sleep for a lifetime and more
for we are finished and done.

The next time you come
floating in from nowhere,
I will snap my fingered thoughts

and drive you out,
I'll turn away and away
and if you dance around me

like a moth in the light
I will aim my strength
at your heart

and drive this stake
right through that part
of our love that still ticks on.

So go home, ghost of love and sleep,
sleep for a lifetime and more
for we are finished and done.

If you come trackless
through the forests
or snaking your way under my door,

if I wake beside you
one more morning,
I'll stab us open to the core

and then you will weep
my shade of love
then you'll weep

follow the winds or
climb a sunshaft to the sky
but turn your shadowy back on me,

and go home, ghost of love and sleep,
sleep for a lifetime and more
for we are finished and done.

LAMENT

These metallic shining tracks may lead us
to those lonely stations that hang in space like bats,
where trains with wild eyes and a whoosh of anonymity
will speed by, and where time will become
at the last, a public clock.

I met you with naive courage on an island that sat
in the ghostly sun, there amongst all the layers of nature,
from flowers to butterflies I chased your elusive energy
as it threaded its careless path
towards dancing strangers and such sorry dawns.

Now defeated and released we clutch tickets to separate
            towns
and our conversation is like one on a worsening telephone
            line,
only our eyes turn occasionally to peer as if shortsighted
into the depths of the other, then memory
like a stilled shot flickers.

Outside the southern country rests flushed with colour
and aloof behind its autumnal window frame.
Enviously I look out locked in my bird cage journey,
still and safe and warm with my fine jagged edge that pleads
silently for the free air and flight and cold chance.

TWO DOORS UP

She hasn't been free from these walled
boundaries of home for seven years,
she talks to me through cold glass;
once she silently held up a photograph
of the man she had loved and lost.

Hers is a hollow life which harbours itself
in our short street,
passing the window you might glance in
to see her sitting over a low fire
wringing her knuckled anxious hands together,

or staring into flames that leap like
troubled memories from the hearth.
The television animates a world
which scares her and she says
she can't be bothered with the papers.

She is built like a thin winter bird,
white and grey and scared, she sits
in the house and waits for visitors
that don't come or is woken restlessly
by ghosts at four a.m.

In one man's view she is nothing
but a fool for not getting out or throwing
aside despair like a jacket
and perhaps in his hard, cold truth
he is right,

or then perhaps one day his world will
crumble too, and finding himself
weeping into a starched pillow
he will come to understand the old woman
two doors up, who never went out.

Paul Munden

THE PRACTICE ROOM

His voice was a stony bass, rinsed
with meths. One side of his cassock
sagged with the tell-tale bottle's weight
and when he leaned across to turn
the page, I was jabbed by the smell.

His hands were yellow ivory, his fingers
exacting hammers. In the dingy practice room
he taught me Hindemith but my progress
was slow, still is. I explained
how I had to divide my time with the violin

at which he took my hands
and felt the flexible knuckles revolve
in their oil. I try it myself now
and it just won't work.

* * *

The room became her Victorian parlour.
She came and went like a ghost,
her grey hair a frizzed silhouette
against the window, beyond which
other boys played cricket in the yard.

She believed in letting the bow ride free.
Before, you had to hold – and later imagine –
a book under the arm. All this

she said in a whispering vibrato
that seemed to brush my skin.

It's been a long time. My violin slides out
from a silk scarf: we uncork the wine.
The piano gives an A for me to crank
the stiff pegs up to the mark.

DANCE

I want you to teach me the waltz.
At school it was always girl
with girl – a fat lot of use.

And worse, dancing was done in gym
which is why my mind pirouettes
to your grey flannel knickers

you kept hidden from matron
embroidered with cress;
better than blotting paper.

We did no dancing at all. Boy
with boy, keeping out of matron's
way, or later, leading her on.

TIE-INS

The plumbing's a doddle he assured me.
It's a question of flow and return.
Look, a diagram.

I remember Slick Vic Richards
who brought gimmicks into chapel –
the British Rail logo turned
on its end to illustrate prayer
being a two-way traffic.

I'm jolted awake by a questionnaire.
I offer my opinion of the restaurant car
– it's all useful feedback – and return
to my book, a new edition to tie in
with the tv series.

O Lord, I pray for a peaceful journey
and a long hot bath.

SOLD

And here's the little kitchen
she'd say as they traipsed through
after her, careful of their heads
on the low ceiling under the stairs.
For some reason I was in tow, moody.
It's not so little. Why little?
I told Dad, maybe to make him cross.
How little I knew. *It's just her way
son, she's very fond of this house.*
By this stage Dad was confined to bed
in the sitting room, which is how
I remembered it and him, with love,
all cramped up.

TEN YEARS ON
(1.5.86)

The Parkstone Road motorcycle shop gleamed
in the sun. Dad and I browsed. In time
I was granted a Honda 50 which lacked
the style I was after, but I rode it
endlessly round the gravel circling
our lawn. Later that summer
it took me away to work on a farm.
This week, scattering seed for grass
of my own, the smell takes me back.
Memories weave. The ground is stitched.

* * *

A few months on I traded the bike
for a 125 with chrome not plastic guards.
Dad's cancer was further advanced
than I knew. He no longer made it out
of doors so I wheeled the bike in
for him to see. I remember my pride
but not what he said. I was impatient;
somehow found the money for a big 250.
I took it fast from Poole to the City
and was lost among the offices, bars.

* * *

For University I kitted myself out
with prestige, a burgundy Harley Davidson,

but soon stepped up to the real, a Triumph,
trimmed in black. I kept it in a bedroom
of our student digs where it didn't leak
a drop. Later though it slackened.
So did I. Riding after pints too many
I clattered off the roof of a swerving car.
My tailored wrist tells the tale. A broken
fingernail still splits as it grows.

* * *

Easy – having worked that macho stuff out
of the blood, writing (to be truthful)
in a nostalgic vein – easy to wish
I'd chosen a less dangerous pursuit,
browsed with Dad, say, for books.
I kept him awake for hours, waiting,
just as his father had done for him
for me to churn the drive, turn the key.
Ten years on my young niece calls him
the one in the gravy. Words fail me too.

Simon Armitage

GREENHOUSE

It's gone to seed now; each loose pane pitted
with lichen like the walls of a fish tank,
the soffits lagged with a fur of cobwebs.
I burst in the other day; kicked the door
out of its warped frame, stood in the green light
among nine years of unnatural growth
and thought back to the morning we built it.
We used the old sash windows from the house,
held them flat with leather gloves, steadied them
down the path. I remember that journey:
you out in front, unsure of your footing
on the damp stones, and me behind counting
each of your steps through our cargo of glass.

Some nights I'd watch from my bedroom window
as you arrived home late from a concert,
and leaving the headlights on to guide you
waded into the black of the garden.
I'd wait, straining for the sound of the hasp
or guessing your distance by the sparkle
of a cufflink. When you disturbed them
the seeds of rosebay willowherb lifted
like air bubbles into the beam of light.
Then you'd emerge, a hoard of tomatoes
swelling the lap of your luminous shirt;
and caught in the blur of double glazing
your perfect ghost, just one step behind you.

VERY SIMPLY TOPPING UP THE BRAKE FLUID

Yes, love, that's why the warning light comes on. Don't
panic. Fetch some universal brake fluid
and a five-eighths screwdriver from your toolkit
then prop the bonnet open. Go on, it won't

eat you. Now, without slicing through the fanbelt
try and slide the sharp end of the screwdriver
under the lid and push the spade connector
through its bed, go on, that's it. Now you're alright

to unscrew, no, clockwise, you see it's Russian
love, back to front, that's it. You see, it's empty.
Now, gently with your hand and I mean gently,
try and create a bit of space by pushing

the float-chamber sideways so there's room to pour,
gently does it, that's it. Try not to spill it, it's
corrosive: rusts, you know, and fill it till it's
level with the notch on the clutch reservoir.

Lovely. There's some Swarfega in the office
if you want a wash and some soft roll above
the cistern for, you know. Oh don't mind him, love,
he doesn't bite. Come here and sit down, Prince. Prince!

Now, where's that bloody alternator? Managed?
Oh any time, love. I'll not charge you for that
because it's nothing of a job. If you want
us again we're in the book. Tell your husband.

WHY WRITE OF THE SUN

when all it has done for us this last year
is dawdle in rain water smeared on the windscreen
or glisten carelessly across drying flagstones.
Take the week of the cottage in Anglesey:
just one afternoon to speak of when we flopped

like synchronised seals into Red Wharf Bay.
Then the drizzle came, the swingball splattered
like a dishcloth and a bike ride to Moelfre
blackened our spines with a plume of dirt.
After three sticky nights we called it a day.

Take the camping weekend under Malham Cove:
drunk with the effort of filling the air-beds
we saw stars spangle in the one-man tent.
Then we slept with a thunderstorm drum-rolling
over us, and dreamt of everlasting happiness

as we drifted apart on the waterlogged groundsheet.
Take the walk along the Humber Bridge
with the wind nagging the high-tension cables.
All we had to time the distance to the waves
was a spent match, and you told me to drop it.

Admittedly, there was one evening; mackerel sky,
this laburnum apparently cascading with yellow
and a breath of air almost saying something
through the trellis. But why write of whispering
when all we ever did that year was shout.

THIS TIME LAST YEAR

From a mile away, the superfine call
of a small girl barely carries itself
to the lawn where we sit. We picture her,
skipping perhaps or swinging a frayed rope
between herself and a fence post till it
wraps around her brother's legs, and jerks her,
drawing out that tiny voice towards us.
Dusk coming on now, slowly, and the roads
and walls give up their heat, just as the pearls
of condensation under the cold-frame
were eased away by the warmth of morning.
Strange, this detail at the two ends of day;
the starting up and slowing down of things.
Nothing now but to go inside; to leave
the wine bottles planted in the growbag,
ignore the football and the broken glass
and forget the cross-cut nap of the lawn,
smudged beyond interpretation. Nothing
but to shake the dead grass from the blankets,
to bundle the deckchairs into the house
and maybe pause in the doorway, watching.
We let the line of fire that ends itself
at the bottom wall of a burned-out field
replace any red sky we had hoped for;
dying as it has done on other nights
against the last hill. And then we lock up.
A thin stream of the cool air from outside
rocks the blind and chills the pillow cases.
We should have closed the windows; already
two moths are battering the bedside lamp,
drawn through the darkness from a mile away,
desperate to be where the only light is.

Adrian Blackledge

WOKEN AT TWO

We lay on our backs in the darkness,
Trying not to hear but picking out
     Sounds: a hoarse, high-pitched plea,
A muffled thud, and something smashing
     Against a car's bumper.

Shouts of vengeance restrained by a third,
Colder voice: 'Come on Col, we've done 'im . . .
     Col!' A pindrop hush, then
Col running back to thud again, each
     Blow bringing a soft *oomph*.

We crept to the blind and caught the bright
Curve of a softball bat falling like
     A lumphammer. There was
Nothing we could do. Walkie-talkies
     Came and went, scratching at

The night's surface. We were shaking and
Sleepless, barely touching, knives glinting
     In an open drawer.
The silence in the street laid us low.
     We might have been the sole

Survivors of an undeclared war;
Children suddenly woken from dreams
     With no one to call to.
Our fingers met and held on, as if
     They could do any good.

47

PHOEBE PEARSALL

'Phoebe Pearsall and Samuel Pearsall, a mere boy and girl . . . were indicted for having at Chilvers Coton on 13th September, endeavoured to conceal the body of a child for the purpose of concealing the birth of the female child of the female prisoner.'
Nuneaton Chronicle, 8 April 1876

They seemed uncomfortable when they came
And wouldn't talk, just stood on the cobbled wharf,
The older one fingering his yellow moustache.
I was still young enough to believe that
All men's moustaches turned yellow with age.
They waited while I shook out the cloth,
Rinsed off the mugs, folded back the table.
Watched as I made up the bunk with blankets,
The younger one shifting from boot to boot,
Not wanting to look. I knew what they'd come for.
While I tidied the cabin it seemed like
This would be the last time. The deathly hush
Hardly breathed as I saw to the embers.
Pain, so much pain. An ammonia stench,
Steam from the chipped bowl. Rain coming in like
God spitting on us. Such desperate pain.
And screaming, screaming but all of it mine.
The older one, the sergeant he must have been,
Helped me from the *Mary* like a gentleman
With his lady. I'd put on my better shawl,
Such as it was, and Mother's cowled bonnet.
I barely noticed his fingers on my arm
As he escorted me. The other
Had brought out cuffs but quickly put them back.
All I could think of while we walked to the town

Was the tiny bundle on the bunk with me
When I woke, wrapped like she was alive.
She followed Sam with her nose; had dry, blue lips.
Sam said some decent words as we slipped her in
Quietly at Chilvers, the September sun
Polishing patches of oil like stained glass.

THE LOOK OF IT
Letters, James Joyce

Do not be offended, dear,
At what I wrote. While I was
Writing my eyes were fixed, as
They are now, on a certain
Word in your letter. There is
Something crude and lecherous
In the very look of it.

The sound of it too is like
The act itself: devilish,
Brutal, irresistible.
You thank me for the new name
I gave you. You see, I am
Something of a poet still
My dark-blue rain-drenched flower.

But inside and side-by-side
This spiritual love is
A craving for every
Mortal inch of your body,
For every secret and
Shameful odour of it, for
Every strange act of it.

I pray to the eternal
Beauty and tenderness in
Your eyes, burst into tears of
Love and pity at a word,
Tremble at a simple chord.
But what I really want is
To lie you down under me.

All I have written above
Is only a moment of
Brutal madness. I love you!
My sweet-eyed blackguard schoolgirl
You are always my lovely
Wild flower of the hedges,
My dark-blue, rain-drenched flower.

DANCING

She's an artist pausing
To consider her art,
Chafed hands on hips, forearms
Clustered with paste-jewel suds.

Already her belly
Is beginning to swell.
The insistent wind in
The linen applauds and

Holding down her printed
Pinafore against it
She seems to take a bow.
Light ricochets from an

Apricot strand as it
Strains from her scarf and she
Tucks it back with two deft
Fingers of her left hand.

She picks up the basket
And in turning glimpses
A flight of Cabbage Whites
Dancing in bleached sunlight.

RENEWAL

Her thighs are dappled as she steps from the bath
And a blackberried silt has settled
In a ring like a recent scar round her neck.

She winds a turban with deliberate hands,
Steals to the centrally-heated bedroom
And kneels to unwrap. The full-length mirror shows

Old strands lit by new flecks and even now
She half expects his click of disapproval.
But the drier blows a sudden rush of warm air,

She grips the brush with dye-stained fingers,
Whispers aloud each precise, downward stroke.
Shakes out more than a mottled bruise of light.

Robert Crawford

SCOTLAND

Glebe of water, country of thighs and watermelons
In seeded red slices, bitten by a firthline edged
With colonies of skypointing gannets,
You run like fresh paint under summer rain.

It is you I return to, mouth of erotic Carnoustie,
Edinburgh in helio. I pass like an insect
Among shoots of ferns, gloved with pollen, intent
On tonguing your meadows, your pastoral Ayrshires, your
        glens

Gridded with light. A whey of meeting
Showers itself through us, sluiced from defensive umbrellas.
Running its way down raincoat linings, it beads
Soft skin beneath. A downpour takes us

At the height of summer, and when it is finished
Bell heather shines to the roots,
Belly-clouds cover the bings and slate cliffs,
Intimate grasses blur with August rain.

HENRY BELL INTRODUCES EUROPE'S FIRST COMMERCIAL STEAMSHIP

Scanning the universe from Helensburgh
You saw the *Comet* first in your own mind
Remote as Egypt, till it crossed the Firth
Blazing a tail of foam and smoke that seemed

Suddenly normal, the future telescoped
From the other shore. Your Cleopatran dream,
Democratised by Watt's technology
Of fire and air, burned on the water and

Made your name History. Not caring about that
A Glasgow girl at the rail accompanied by
Two sets of radial paddles whistled to her man
Choruses from Allan Ramsay's *The Ever Green*.

JOHN LOGIE BAIRD

You're everywhere fleetingly through the Nipkow discs
As if you were photographing yourself asleep
Which you did in Helensburgh. Paternal, the Clyde's slow
    Raj
Plugged East Argyle Street into *The Golden Bough*
And howled down your phones whose tree-strung, complex
    cables
Unseated a bus driver. There's still no comment

Explains why when it rained past Dumbarton Rock
You evaded classics for *The Boys' Book of Pastimes*
And pre-empting the Wright Brothers. Finding at an
    exchange
Between centuries, leading electric light
Into the manse, one dreich day you discovered
Yourself, grown tottery in the sodden garden

When hydrangeas shook blooms into fibre-optics,
Your own invention. Brilliant, bronchial, thin
You shared hard schooldesks with Reith, J., and Bonar Law
The Canadian orphan. A dominie lochgellied you once
For pronouncing 'eelensburgh' like those wild, untouchable
    tinks
Who if they could see your whole career from today's

Long distance, would say, 'Christ! that boay's done weel
Wha's faither kent aboot Eastern relijuns.' Blood-transmitter
Of Irish kings, Glasgow MAs, and Creole
West Indian songs, screened from douce cousins,
Under bamboos at a small jam factory
Near Port of Spain you achieved television

Like a kind of love, seeing as far as linking
Continents together, and you paid for it.
'That will be all . . .' At your trials the now *Lord* Reith
Sent you away, a schoolboy with a thousand lines set
To define the most accurate pictures ever shown,
Your punishment exercise. Cramped-up on rickety chairs

You were bombed out. When World War Two ended
Baird equipment broadcast victory in the Savoy
But not one diner said 'Cheerio' when you faded,
A white coded enigma, blandly edited out,
Coughing away down the water towards Trinidad, beaming
In secret triumph over those Clydelike waves.

THE SCOTTISH NATIONAL CUSHION SURVEY

Our heritage of Scottish cushions is dying.
Teams of careful young people on training schemes
Arrived through a government incentive, counting
Every cushion. In Saltcoats, through frosty Lanark.
They even searched round Callanish
For any they'd missed. There are no more Scottish cushions
Lamented the papers. Photographs appeared
Of the last cushion found in Gaeldom.
Silk cushions, pin cushions, pulpit cushions.
We must preserve our inheritance.
So the museums were built: The Palace of Cushions, the
      National
Museum of Soft Seating, and life went on elsewhere
Outside Scotland. The final Addendum was published
Of *Omnes Pulvini Caledonii.*
Drama documentaries. A chapter closed.
And silently in Glasgow quick hands began
Angrily making cushions.

MR AND MRS WILLIAM MULOCK
IN THE MUSEUM OF ETHNOLOGY

Mr Mulock, staring at
The gaps between the hieroglyphs,
Shuffles his feet, and wonders what
His wife sees in that row of stiffs

Embalmed in old stone coffins. She
Is rapturous. 'The guide book said
"All visitors must go and see
The fertile Nile's immortal dead"

And now we have.' The husband coughs
But smiles to please his cultured wife:
Lost in the Pharaohs' autographs,
She disregards a common life.

Woman and man, each stands and seems
Odd, undeciphered, quite alone.
Surrounded by elusive dreams.
Fragments of the Rosetta Stone.

Gwyneth Lewis

DALTON'S GERANIUM*

in shocking-pink blossoms and brilliant green ruff
shook as he carried her earthenware pot
to the workroom table, where he set it down,
the better to see her. They gathered round,

looking intently at the bright, loud blooms
nodding, indulgent of three men's stares.
Dropped petals clashed with the red felt cloth
but were left there, while each friend considered in turn

what colour he saw there. Deep salmon, was it?
Or light cerise? Three parts red
to two parts blue? Dark coral, tinged
with an orange hue – or red-tinted cyclamen?

Someone jolted the table as they fumbled for names,
making her quiver, though they all agreed
she kept faith with one colour, although colour-fast words
they had none, for all of the fleshed-out shades

they had lavished upon her. Dalton was silent,
dressed in mis-matched clothes. He turned the pot slowly,
then blushed as he said that to him she was fickle,
that his name for pink changed from sky blue by day

to deep red by night. By his lights, blood
flowed bottle green; fires burned viridian
and a sepia sun hung over everything.
Made cuckold to colour by his faithless eyes!

But his dunned world had doubly ravished him
and sighted blindness made him lust the more
the more he was cheated. Much later, alone,
he was drawn again to his vivid plant

standing inscrutable, smelling faintly of soil.
He made to replace her, lingered, then touched
the amber circles on the yielding leaves,
hungry for colour in her dusky dyes.

*John Dalton (1766–1844), the discoverer of the Atomic Theory, was the
first scientist to describe the phenomenon of colour blindness, which he
noticed because of the defect in his own vision.

THE BAD SHEPHERD

Cornelius Varro knows his husbandry
and he maintains a flourishing estate:
My mutes stand guard at the entrance gate.
Vowels I lodge with my hired men,
half-vowels sit by the cattle pen.
Of course, I let the spirants work the field,
as they're teaching the clover how to yield
to consonantal chimings from the church.
But I'm uncouth, and keep lip service back.

For I'm the one who herds his fields of wheat,
speaks softly till the stalks are white,
the ripe ears heavy. Then I sow my spite
and laugh to see how the rows stampede,
as I spread sedition with the highland wind
till they're wrecked and broken. Then he sends men round
and I watch in silence as they slowly reap
his yearly tribute from my grudging ground.

IN THE SNOW QUEEN'S PALACE

It is winter again, and she thinks of Kay
in a city apartment where the light is cold
and he's in his shirtsleeves watching the display

on his computer screen. Though he's silent,
he's shifting round glowing blocks of words
as if he'd forgotten what they could have meant,

or who could have sent them, because now he sees
patterns more lovely than the real thing
in his own arrangements. Soon his breath will freeze

on the inside of the window panes. His eyes
are polar. Ask him, he'll say that he's doing fine,
everything's dandy. But his life's on ice

and a thaw could break him. Avoiding pain
takes concentration and he's lost belief
in simple summer. She will not visit him again.

A WELCOME TO EAST OXFORD

Since I heard that you moved into Bartlemas Close
I've stopped feeling mopish and lachrymose
at the thought of you playing so hard to get –
the Big Man On Campus in the stylish set –
because I've great faith in this neighbourhood.
The pubs are so-so, but the Elm Tree's good.
Like it or not, now I'm on your map,
for our comings and goings will overlap.
You see, since you moved down the Cowley Road,
we've got masses in common (well, the postal code
just for starters) and we're bound to meet,
say at the cinema that's on Jeune Street,
or going to Tesco's or the laundromat,
where you'll have to be nice and stop for a chat.
There's a tattoo centre past the bingo hall
and the blue compartments in the Prince of Bengal
are just perfect for dining *tête-à-tête*,
for an informal curry, say that we met
by chance late one evening . . . But if this is all wrong
and my fantasy's coming on far too strong –
I wouldn't want to put you on edge –
I'd settle for Divinity Fruit and Veg
now and then in the morning as you pick up your bread.
The Patels will think I've gone soft in the head.
I won't pester or bug you, but since I heard
that you moved into Bartlemas Close on the third
I don't see the street, but a *mise-en-scène*
for a loving liaison, a backdrop for when
you will finally grant the attention due
to one who adores you in Fifty-Two.

Michael Symmons Roberts

THE BOTANICAL GARDENS

The Botanical Gardens are closed
For the winter. The beds are all black.
The shrubs are sprung like wire traps.
Through the scrollwork gates we see
The vanilla-painted ice-cream house
Being licked dirty by the rain.

The tide has deserted the marine lake.
The peacocks have been stuffed
And boxed, their tails now hats and fans.
The empty wire coops rattle
Out of shape. The last of the season's
Bread swells and melts uneaten.

Only the glasshouse keeps its insides
Green. Water runs like a brass rail
Through it, air too rich to breathe.
Our gloves have frozen to the gates.
All we can see of the glasshouse
Is a jet of smoke from across the lake.

THE ICED CANAL

Birds flew in black seams from the field
Where they were feeding. Their wings beat
Like cloth pulses, and the cold seed spilled
Down over us, too fat to hold in a beak.

We stepped and slithered on the brim
Of the iced canal. We threw dead sticks
Which broke or blemished the snow skin,
Revealing the dark where ice and water mix.

I wandered out, and plummeted through
A crack where water had begun to bleed
Up through the ice. You watched, then flew
For the trees with your lips trailing seed.

THE ALLOTMENT

In the mornings I wake, walk and dig.
In the afternoons I cut and dry;
Evenings I consume.
I am the one with caked root hands
And dry black nails.
This is the muck I was born from, into;
It is here that I prepare the ground
To take me whole, so I can be the soil
That dries on your youthful,
Burrowing fingers.

This is the open, naked girl
Ripped from a magazine left
On the allotments. My digging
Was delayed by rain, I watched her
Mouth fill up with water,
And her legs, funnelling.
She held a look of ecstasy
As I spaded her into the mud;
Fuel for later.

I like to get here early
Before the others come.
The dogs come first and then
The hollow rumbling of empty barrows.
By the time they arrive
My patch is like a jungle
I have soil as rich as blood.
It is slicking sweetly through my veins.

This is the child who's been
Missing since . . .
This is the child who was
Beaten lifeless left in a quiet river,
Washed up onto the edge of the soil.
I had seen her running away
With the man whose cold hands
Were printed on her neck when I found her.
Within a day she was part of my soil.
Her crop was young, fresh and green.
For a whole day the allotment
Burst and was cut.
The girl rose through my tending,
Then there was nothing – barren.

I am the man who can tame the earth,
Can make it rise through
My little patch of ground.
My spade is charmed.
Every dusk I wheel a mountain home,
Of skin and bones.
Flesh for the sleepless.
Smokeless fuel for the quiet man's night.

SCRAP METAL

The whinings of light planes
half-wake me. In my sleep-half,
the sky fills with so many
that their wings clack together
like beaks, bringing them down
in the field behind the house.

The rooks in the end trees
racket amongst themselves.
The house shifts on its rust
mattress of scrap metal.
The soil beneath is gorged
with bolts, chains and spokes.

I tear off finger-long strips
of the blue-and-gold-patterned
wallpaper by the bed. Underneath,
the old paint feels cold.
I decide to paint my room
Completely orange – windows too.

The hill in the rooks' field
is a long-barrow for motorbikes.
Sometimes in the night,
I hear one spark up
like a distant throat,
then settle again.

THE CANOEIST

Standing in July,
but thinking about winter,
I froze the Kennet and Avon Canal.
It spread like cramp from where I stood
and seized the surface, stilling it.

I peopled it too, some walked,
some shoe-skated. Even boats grew
where I pictured them – frozen in
against the banks, tarpaulined over –
that stiff too.

Moving wider, trees were stripped,
left black except the branch tips –
them frozen, and the fields scythed, burnt,
empty – back roads closed.

I thought I'd finished and was turning
away when I saw a canoeist
coming out of the distance,
trailing July behind him.

I held my ground, he thawed it
as he stepped on to the bank, carried
his canoe like an enormous hat
beyond the lock, and set off again,
dismantling my winter.

Paul Henry

COUNTRY HEADMASTER

In church, you sing to be heard
by the less assertive voices.
On straying to another key
the organ follows you.
Where others pause for breath,
your vibrato fills in.

And back out in the sunlight,
you're an ologist of all that lives
and is dead about you in the yard.
Clever sod. A dishevelled world
has shrunk to the whim of your brain,
assembles itself neatly there.
You can name any flower,
bird, leaf or river
in almost any language.
When you smile, it's God
on the smug, seventh day.
Nobody comes near you.

Your big white house overlooks
an eager stretch of water
trying too hard for the sea.
I've caught you there, all boy,
tongue-tied, your crooked hand
stuttering flat stones
across to the other side.

RETIRED

The house, with all its edges
and corners and hollow comforts
has grafted itself onto them,
the coral on the fish.
As much as love can be is theirs.
Pawn love, moving within defensible squares,
my father's his creaking chair,
the fireplace, the coal bunker,
hers the posh kitchen with its gadgets
ticking on and off all day.

He plays the piano for her to sing
the same old songs of love and dying,
he the rock and she the river round it.
Her sharp notes, his awkward chords,
are scaling back upstream to snatch
a ripple of the first splash
of music they made together.
They swim back now too often
against the grain of time,
spout the same old anecdotes.

Careful as they are, they don't fear
the empty grate, the quiet kitchen.
They smile and carry on
and go to chapel every Sunday,
he guarding the fire that dries
the clothes she'll wash on Monday.

WIDOWS OF TALYLLYN

They lived as needed, hid their strength,
survived the male, modestly,

block the aisle on the market bus,.
still see husbands in summer fields,

still wear rings on mortal fingers,
grasp cupfuls of chipped memories,

wake at sober dawns and leave
their precious days unsquandered.

CWM DYFFRYN*
for Glyn 'Sharky' Price

Respectable now, my pale hands
direct the hoover's plough,
ejecting from the carpet
the crumbs between its furrows.

Its drone becomes a tractor's,
fifty miles, ten years away,
gritting its teeth in the earth,
unlocking them shining.

You had sentenced me to stones,
to wade in each new wound
spurting red in your wake
and clear its clotted throat.

One hour stretched me out
on the rack of my spine
to my limit and I snapped,
dug deep in the soil

for an unstitched pocket
embroidered with worms,
hooked you from your element
with worms, your biggest fear.

The Massey-Ferguson rolled on
into the dark without you.
Only the late birds caught
our laughter in that valley.

74

Respectable now, my pale hands
unplug such incidents,
the characters of dust
ascending in a silent room.

*Dyffryn Valley, South Powys.

THE WALK TO WORK

Early blue above terraces.
Even the brimming skips
exhibit their loads brilliantly
in what sculpture the sun
has made of a grey town.

Five lollipop women march
to different centre stages,
mime soliloquies of children
to anonymous, dark shapes
giving way to the scurry.

Blue morning up for grabs.
Sheer blue fly sheet
the chimneys peg down,
barbed wire wings tear,
shavings of planes smear.

Louder by the corner now,
the traffic's mad till
cashing in and out
its small change of lives,
quickening pedestrian minds.

Cracked paving stones underfoot
duplicate by the streetful
grave, type-set expressions.
Already a simple blueprint
crumples itself into cloud.

David Morley

FOUR POEMS TO MY FATHER

HEIRLOOM

Two lines on an envelope twine
like frost – my father's poetry

There's no date to tell
if between courtship and counselling

he snicked his wrist of verse.
All I recall is the swarf

where he worked,
plumes of acetylene,

ghost-chatter of lathes . . .
not this: this cutting

the metal of speech,
commas like weld-scars;

his life-work with steel:
a rounding

rounding of an icicle.

IN LOCO PARENTIS

There is a dust settling in you
like that on a ledge.
We plane it away thickly yet
it binds like earth.
You cannot enter
in our esteem more
that now you trail behind
like a shattered hawk,
hard-ribbed readiness
in hunger of us.

We know you, you do not know,
as if, mercifully,
your ruins had sealed humility;
it is no shame to vomit before children.
Indeed your own will clean you after,
they will prepare and dress you.
In death they will cling like roundworm
until, mouth wiped and lungless,
you emerge, immured in permafrost,
from your speckled bed.

ERRAND

I came to a place where buildings were going up;
biscuits of slate sat wrapped in twine.
Earth moved like sugar, boiling
against the metal of a dumper.
A machine dropped, dropped its yellow snout,
nuzzling at joists
it hammered-in.
When I got to my father I would learn

the heat of that impact, how you might
light paper from it two hours on . . .
The air meanwhile would shiver with fire,
a fineless dust, the shouts of impact.

He was with the welders –
short-term hire – cutting thin plate
to microns. Not visored, he
stood out from that coven
of kneeled and sparking men
like something they were making
or melting to start over.
We went out to sandpiles, pounded stone,
his eyes spindling, his mouth
asking and asking why I was there.

METAL-WORK

The lathe we were at
kept cutting-out
in little deaths;
our anger slid.

Under a blade
sheet-metal split.
I stood where
my father stood me:

this side of a lathe.
Weathers of dust
fell to a hush
at my feet.

I did what he asked:
watched calipers twitch
legs skinny,
an avocet's;

but looked beyond:
to drill-heads primed,
fluted like wands
of steel.

He halved the work:
held mandrels, clamp.
Drills spoke for him,
talked themselves out.

MARDALE HEAD

A reservoir, filling, cut
out a village in a flag of grey,
haloing folds, indulging walls
their done-with labour. Thud

at the damstone, a door slammed shut.
Then they grieved for sheep still out:
wily beggars slipping collie-dog nets.
Compensation came like drizzle on water

and wouldn't add . . . A stop-go track
lopes up to nothing: the dam,
its forehead half blown-off. Winds relevel
what water-blades cancel:

stove, trellis, the twines of washday.
Now, as this osprey confuses
surface and fishlight, skylines
narrow, a tightening wire,

precarious with fresh weather.

CLIMBING ZERO GULLY
for P.C., killed on Ben Nevis, 1982

There is no cut rock
but terrified stones
keeping the peace,
unchallenging.

They challenge:
perusing second-pitch belay,
scribing snake-backs in the snow,
hard as glacier,

the piton correcting itself
almost self-consciously.
Hand and over-hand, they jerk
upwards and on,

absolutely competent, nursed
by Japanese equipment.
On comes a night,
bleating, unchallenging.

Rock: screw-faced and water-brained.
They: complete in mountain-power
stand, chin in hand,
suddenly vigilant.

Katrina Porteous

FACTORY GIRL

Five nights a week I work as a factory girl.
My job's in Necklaces. Cartons of colourful beads
Run down the line and I thread them. The Sorter leads,
Popping them into their boxes – a difficult task,
For sometimes the green look blue, the blue look black,
And many fit all six boxes equally well;
But the Sorter has to be certain they don't get mixed.
Everything's made to fit. The order's fixed,
See, by the day, and we stick to it, or else
There's plenty others wanting jobs . . .
                                        My shift's eleven
At night till the early morning bell drills seven
Into my dreaming. Then I go home to bed.
I don't know whether it's dark or light out there.
In here it's always the same, summer or winter.
With all of our necklaces made to the book, as we thread
In the given order (green today, then red;
Tomorrow red, then green), to me they appear
So much the same; like the nights, the bus ride here,
The sequence of stop after stop, long as the Tyne,
Counting the lights in the water, the broken line
Down where the shipyards were that went redundant.

I think of the oddest things to unsettle the pace:
Sometimes of Dad. I try to remember his face
And the stories my mother told me: ('You should've seen
How he looked in his uniform, Hin, when he went to the
          War!
I don't think I'd ever loved him so much before.

83

What a knees-up we had when the fighting was over! At last
We were done with the sirens, the blackouts and rations.
    God willing,
He'd still have his job at Swan Hunters'. But that was gone.
'When he heard, he looked like a factory shutting down,
The lights going out in the workshops, one by one . . .').

Well, I string this together. I try to make sense of the past.
But pieces are all I have. I can't force them to mean
Anything much. I just see what I want to. It seems
An haphazard collection of memories, turned in the telling
This way or that by a whim, as an order's cast;
O, nothing seems to make logical sense any more.
I go home, and I dream of necklaces snapping, beads spilling
Into their moving millions, over the floor.

IF MY TRAIN WILL COME

If my train will come
Quietly, in the night,
With no other sound than the slow
Creak of wheel upon wheel;
If, huge as a house but brighter,
Crouched at the edge of the fields
Like a steaming beast, it is waiting
Down the deserted road;
Though the colliery gate and the church
Where my mother and father were wed
Are all grown over at last
And the people I knew there dead now,
If a stranger alights
And holding my breath, I see
That he has your eyes, your hair,
But does not remember me;
And if there follows a girl
With my face from years ago
And for miles by the side of the tracks
The Durham grasses blow –
O, if my train will come
With its cargo of souls who have passed
Over this world to find me,
Will I go? Will I want to?

GONE AGAIN

Gone again.
As though the sea had tangled him
Up in its white mesh, breathing evenly,
Trawling him out to go down at the edge of the sky.

Day after day
I have watched them vanishing
Into the crack which the days are delivered from,
Wave after wave of them, small boats, sliding away.

If he never comes back again –
If in its suck and tumble the sea will not mother him
But filling our footprints forever, the sand has short
        memory –

I think that the weight of all this time without him
Will float me east with the small boats, laden, one evening,
To cleave the sea from the sky and buffet between them

And reel in the long, sad past on a single line.

DUCKS

In their beady dreams among sleepy green sluices,
Water slopping on walls and prim willows,
After a long day's leisurely wallowing,
Niggling, bickering – could they be envious,

Those sleek Cambridge ducks in their comfortable couples:
Pompous in uniform, aggressively sociable,
Well-stuffed with breadcrusts, insufferably jolly,
Awkward on land, on ice, skittled, ridiculous?

Here on the hush of a tide, the seasons' drifting,
Lone Northumbrian eiders dumbly endure
The creeping to bitterness, death-cold and thaw,
Dipping and riding the heave like rafts.

It's said they're the souls of the drowned cast back,
Free. Like the hermit saint their shag-wings warmed,
No ice-flurry ruffles their sea-bound calm.
They gather in darkness. Under the storm's assault,

Buffeted into knots, they stay; then leaving
No ties, in spring the drakes straggle off in brave,
Vain male huddles, pied surf on black basalt.
She'll raise her brindled brood in the bent alone,

The brown mother eider, minding a neighbour's clan
In shifts; till soon, into the steep grey waves
She'll pitch her tiny, trusting, buoyant crop
Of woolly ducklings, wildly rocked to sleep.

DIFFERENCES
Concord, Massachusetts

At Concord they decided their differences.
She strode ahead among the ancient trees.
He watched her angry back. Eyes watched him watching –
Snakes, frogs, mice, chipmunks, under the leaves.
He wished that he was home in downtown Boston
Among the paved arcades and galleries.

On the Old North Bridge he held her tightly.
The water slipped relentlessly away,
Cool green, opaque and sluggish. He could not fathom
What it was that seemed different about her today.
Her English primness letting him no further,
She glared into the river, would not say.

She did not recognise her own reflection.
Her thoughts looked older. Knuckled roots of oak
Told lies of home, familiar but foreign
As all bold Boston youths. She felt the ghosts,
Unnumbered soldiers, wake; and cold foreboding,
The Redcoat's sweaty terror, gripped her throat.

'Will you go back,' he asked, 'or stay?' The birds were silent.
She sensed the soldiers' voices in the calm
Hushing of the maples. He heard nothing.
The squirrels shivered in the treetops. Harm –
Hurt of the water snake, the farmer's bullet –
Drew close. He felt town calling him; she, home.

Gerard Woodward

SUFFOLK INTERIOR

And when the brass vase she stole
From Stoke-by-Nayland
Was placed on the dresser

My brother restole it and sold it for scrap.
And when we lowered the venetian blinds
The kitchen was filled with belfry light.

And I remember the infinities of my train set
With the engine furiously figure-eighting
And whose motor smelt of struck flint.

And so my mother's theft made our house
A church, the bench ends of the chair backs
Felt like knee skin of a child that falls often.

And my father under the ellipse of the lamp shade,
Haloed well in reading, knuckles
Digging into the folded wings of his cheek bones,

And the aftermath of the washing up
Where St Catherine's leper water
Cooled in the red basin,

And the darkness that stayed in the loft
That was roofed in slate slotted
Like feathers on a rook's back

And all the shadows were so old
That if you were to remove the walls
You would have a house of dark air still standing.

MAIDEN VOYAGE

You said my blood contained salt.
Saxa Sam sailing through my veins.
And then you told me of all your captains,
My Great Grandfather, the one

With the hook, who I look like,
Who took coal from Newcastle to Tilbury
In a ship nicknamed *The Coffin*
After the many times it had sunk,

How he delivered gifts to your mother
In his younger days; a rug
From somewhere out east,
An icon from Archangel

Painted by real Russian hands,
Both now lost.
You wept for all your dry sons.
Your tears did have some salt at least.

And so I decided to do a Conrad,
Left school early to join the Merchant Navy.
They sent me letters
With little red flags in the corner.

You became worried but came with me
On my interview. My eyes were tested
By a man who conjured the sea
In his tiny office

By switching off the light.
Coloured pinpoints appeared.
They were the lights of ships
Four miles distant;

Green, red, blue, white.
A dark breeze crossed his clinic ocean,
I stood up and walked on water
And drank all seven seas from a plastic tumbler.

Captain Skull told me it would be dangerous
For me to be on the high seas
With the asthma I hadn't had for three years.
I could see you were relieved,

Your pendant swung like an anchor.
But I had got the colours right.
Perhaps it is best that I went to art school
In the long run.

LOFT WATER

I was frightened
Of the loft's lightness.
In case it floated off

I wanted it tethered there,
Filled with a ballast
Of history, aerials and water.

Perhaps it was foolish
To drink from its tank
And risk the weight

Of the whole thing decreasing,
But on hot nights
I could not help

Swallowing until it hurt,
Water as cold
As if from earth.

And I sank into bed
As bloated as a fish,
Heavy with liquid

But still a dangerously light anchor
For that kite of slate
I flew in sleep.

THE SECRET BATHROOM

I have learned the names of the rooms,
But what is this one called,
The one whose door is locked?

Like the kitchen it contains water,
I can hear it,
But, I suspect, no knives.

Is it another bedroom?
If so, who sleeps in it?
We are all counted for

In this house
And I would fear a stranger
Plumping up unknown pillows.

If it is a living room
Why is it locked?
To live needs no secrecy,

Just chairs and ornaments.
I cannot remember if this door
Has ever been open.

Then the person in there
Must be starving
To death.

It sounds enormous
The way it echoes,
Worse than a church.

Perhaps it is a door
To the outside, upstairs,
Opening to a fall through trees.

But there is a lake in there
And someone swimming
In a hot, flowery summer.

And I notice that all
The walls, ceilings and floors
Of the house are flowing

With rivers as if all
Were melting as an igloo thaws
To a pool of liquid house.

But now I hear this woman's voice
Speaking like a mermaid from the water,
Reminding me how I was once a fish

In her lake, when she,
With her rope of blood,
Angled me out.

Jonathan Davidson

EPITHALAMIUM

I think we've reached the point
of slowing down and so to marrying;
bracing ourselves in our slovenly ways
to catapult our features to the future,
to be the parents of unhappy children.

Simon, Richard, Mark are marrying
to secure for ever decent replication
of their surnames, to make it safe to die –
which is odd as they never spoke to me
of a craving for immortality.

So they wrestle with reproduction
and I wrestle with words, both acts
not overrun with romance and probably,
when it is all over and we turn to sleep,
surprisingly devoid of strong emotion.

TWO CYCLISTS

I

My Dad and I
used to ride out south
cycling with the Cycling Club
on Sundays – or on our own –
over the hills and – you guessed it –
far away.

Once we found
strawberries and once
we found a watch still ticking.
We often found rabbits
and sometimes pigeons
and great blackberries.

II

When the last spoke
has broken and the last
seat-pin has painfully snapped
we'll burn our maps and shake clean
our memories of summer to summer.
And we'll carry ourselves out –
while there's hardly light in the sky –
and dump ourselves in the field of wheat
or in the beautiful, autumnal,
metallic clump of beech trees on the hill.

MOVING THE STEREO

We screwed the transit screws down tightly
and clipped the needle arm into its cradle
and carried it down like a kid's coffin,

only it rattled and was too heavy.
Stuck on the stairs I could hear myself say:
Let's leave it, put it back into its place

between the single bed and the boxes
of hi-fi magazines. And lowering it
into your car's boot it caught my finger –

surely a sign – and there was no plaster.
At the house we clashed on where to put it
but with only one socket it always was

up against the TV set – your parents'
generous gift. It was while selecting
a compact disc to wet the baby's head with –

so to speak – that pulling the plug on tact
you told me in so many words to grow up,
though it was *my* stereo and I never

cared for your collection. So it was late
when sick of circling we each uncoiled
a speaker from its lead and faced the music.

THE TRAIN SPOTTER

Rather a timid child. Not good with girls
I chose the track-side life but never cleared
my Thirty-Threes or saw a Western gallop
westward with the Cheltenham Spa Express –
a wildcat bobbing through the Wiltshire dust,
hydraulic paws punching loose fishplates.
I came too late or peaked too soon or something.

Once on a day-trip to York I did see
one of the last Deltics – I forget which –
but it roared like an oven and its wheels
squealed like a sack of kittens as it bit
its solid way south with a slow parcels.
As I tell the new lot, that was a real
sleepless-nights-of-wanting locomotive.

THE GARDEN

I stalk the raspberries feeding myself.
My sister is in the blackcurrants.
In fifteen minutes' time she will be sick,
violently sick in the coal bunker.
The coal bunker has lost its coal
to gas central heating throughout
and we hide in it. It is our pit,
our mine shaft. It descends deep
beneath the dandelion scrub
of the lawn, beneath the dying
crab-apple tree, beneath the fence
enclosing our smallholding.
It travels to a depth at which
we cannot smell the stink of sick
or see the legendary blue sky
or feel our grubby hunters' hands
across our eyes, or hear our tongues
babbling numbers for the hide and seek.
We only know the sudden shadow-cold,
the woodlice squashed by our sandals,
the red eggs of the spiders bursting,
the red bricks spiralling, black with coal,
and the long tunnel of afternoons
pelting into the future like stones
lobbed by bullies at our faces.

Nicholas Drake

THE DISAPPEARING CITY
Prague, 1938/London, 1988

The disappearing city in her head
has street names blanked; façades fall to the wind
and cobblestones in waves shine under rain.

One street still stands, and at the top she lives
by a window, closed, unshattered; the last one
of a city of windows waiting for the sun.

Zigzags where stairs once led. A golden grove
by a black river. Snow falls in the night.
She is a gargoyle stone hunched in the eaves

in company with lions and angels, carved
leaping the walls and arches, their moss eyes
pecked out by all the wintering birds she loved.

But they have flown away, and the dark doors
stand open to the cold, old enemy
who loots eggs, children, music, cakes and flowers.

At dawn the storm troops execute the clocks;
birthdays, deathdays, anniversaries
are secrets which her dreaming heart unlocks

once in a while or once upon a time
now she is blind, and spring, shot in the back,
has fallen down into a pit of lime.

The door is bolted. Liars shout at her
from the next room. The lift whirrs up and down
inexplicably, each stop an error.

Phone off the hook; the new directories
of a foreign city; *a stranger has no name;*
the numbers are all wrong; no one is home.

Upon the pillow her dandelion head
which time has breathed upon, is gently laid
awake and listening to the radio's crack and hiss;

voices, languages, somewhere a lost tune
for chandelier and dancer, long ago;
a midnight waltz, round and around, alone.

THE PIGEONS IN WENCESLAS SQUARE
(August 1968/August 1988)

This is the capital of Absurdistan:
at six o'clock, the upright hour of newscasts
and whistling birds, the sweep of seconds stalled
in Wenceslas Square the day's shadows of rain,
and a pin let drop could be heard in the radio silence
with its crowd of angels falling to the stones.

The future ghosts of social engineers
vanished along 'Defence of Peace' to the airport
with convalescents just home from the Black Sea;
the Arrivals and Departures boards
unspelt the names of cities and other times:
HAVANA, DAMASCUS, VIENNA, LONDON, blank.

Pigeons occupied the empty square,
puzzled on parapets and statues' heads,
by windows of castles and palaces from which
governments had fallen or been pushed;
in the architecture of finance and flags
pigeons in stone tiers, row upon row.

Now restoration is a gift of love,
as when a worker on the nation's ceiling,
among the clichés and the chandeliers,
like St Wenceslas his coins, the city's stars,
scattered a history book of pure gold leaves
on the vacant auditorium below.

LOCAL HISTORY

I

The Romans first lit beacons on this point
of land backed by a marsh, face to the sea;
a kingdom of bright fires, 'Island of Light'.

No stones were set to mark a pilgrim quest;
the ways sank without trace; the maps retreat
to shrines in ports and cities further west

where miracles were not confused with storms,
Leviathans that feasted upon ships,
the bones and bells beneath the shifting calms,

but inland homed like swallows to the eaves,
to glass and gargoyles in the masonry,
and golden cocks on spires, and sudden leaves.

II

The railways made the stations at the sea
an end in sight, like summer; every year
by generations came the families

to pleasure gardens, gentry balconies,
Shell Grotto and the Dreamland cinema –
most famous of the picture palaces

that once were Zion chapels and dance halls.
Gulliver's England; giant and child alike
kick down the castles, ride the Biggest Wheels:

Punch and Judy, the pier-head's shiny bands
and Christy Minstrels singing to the bones;
a diver cyclist riding with no-hands

nonchalance like a po-faced Icarus
unfeathered, hopeless, falling to the waves
and the bathchair dreamers' slow, insane applause.

III

Photographs pose father each July,
black shoes and socks with mother, paddling
before the war, and after, with the boy,

his Western Desert hidden in the dunes.
Strange relations taken 'pleasant please',
chairs sunk in sand, all staring at the sun

like a brilliant balloon, a miracle,
and smiling, maybe, at Britannia –
Aphrodite waving from her shell;

drawn by seahorses to the golden sand
she smilingly distributes £5 notes
and long-lost loved-ones' messages by hand . . .

Tintype shadows in the vinegar bath;
the telescopes' confusion, coin by coin;
faceless mermaids and sailors, shoddy mirth.

IV

British Summer Time, its floral clock
a thirteenth hour of freedom and local
histories of ice-cream and seaside rock.

In the green iron and glass pavilion
a tramp beneath a blanket, derelict,
like Rip Van Winkle in the chantry sun

and this his ocean dream, a gentle trick
or failed shrine none in winter visit now
unless, like us, to stay one night and wake

early to deserted esplanades,
a window light among the windless squares,
the tide returned to sky and perfect sands;

in the silent dining rooms on Ocean Road
compass suns on charts and ships in bottles
on a sea like the mirror's quicksilver, becalmed.

Lavinia Greenlaw

RESISTANCE

At eight, dirty old men got boring
so, short of a slug to salt,
we set out to reclaim the playground.
Listless for adventure, we quarried a stranger,

slope-shouldered and alone. The hunt was on.
No matter which path he took we were there
confronting him with cotton dresses.
This was a man with a woman's voice, pleading.

What did we want?
The one in the bushes had wanted
the way to the toilets.
The one in Menorca had wanted

to show me lizards in his garden
but nutcrackered my buttocks
in loose leather palms.
What did we want?

To hound him off the heath, to skip
along the pavement, for once forgetting
the cracks. Every time he looked back
we were still – but we were still there.

I can remember his words, his face,
and when the fever broke: our eyes caught
by a heat-crazed puppy that slipped its lead
to seduce each passing leg.

The sun blooded our foreheads
in sweat or celebration
as we faced the long walk home
up a short ladder, down a long snake.

NORTH

That skin wasn't made for this weather
and cannot be cured. It retains
the softness of a new bruise.

Only your hands reveal the pull
of an eight-mile post round over the hills,
leaving clues house by house.

Seventy miles to town once a month
for things that don't need a fridge.
In between there is bread and bread.

Sheep sit in the road causing accidents.
One swerves past, tripping over its guts
in the panic to find a way out.

That dog will be shot by a man
who cleans the heel of his boot
on the purple palace of a jellyfish.

The river's lifeline pins a mountain down
and feeds you yellow flowers
that spill from your front door

but what I hold in my heart is your son,
star-blond on the seashore,
his hands full of stone

that could never be a perfect round
but will dress itself in circles
as it breaks the water and breaks the water.

Your landscape reads like a palm that held ice.

A CHANGE IN THE WEATHER

They drive to the beach at Seatown, easily
entering a scene that the winter light
has overcast with single shades of grey
and brown – old like an old painting.
The child finds the curled fist of an ammonite
and traces its shape with each plump finger,
curious at something so round and so dead.
The man explains about the failure to adapt;
how the shell can give up its flesh

then fill each pore with grains of sand
until it turns to stone. The woman walks on
(there is a way of leaving but staying
in sight). Her child runs to give her this,
the only still thing in a shifting world
where land becomes sea then Seatown beach
where she tries to fit her hand to the curves
and studies the clouds, not knowing their names
but looking for a change in the weather.

AN ANALYST'S DIVORCE

'Individual acts in which one kills
knowingly are the exception' (Wilhelm Reich)

Four children keep an appointment
with their parents and a stranger
in a living room that has always been
too big. It gets avoided.

The mother places herself under siege
and disappears like a spotless glass
arranged in shadow, while her husband
of twenty-three years sits behind

an invisible desk and takes comfort
in the cleansing power of theory.
His training permits the expression of grief
and anger, so each child gets five minutes.

The eldest has travelled a hundred miles
with his fists clenched and ready
but the stranger has honeyed the room
with kind tones to protect the furniture

and the son remembers how at school
he couldn't stop hitting his friends
so the teacher confiscated his shoes
and forced mittens onto his furious hands.

The first daughter feels her bowels melt.
It crosses her mind to shit on the carpet
as this would be of professional interest
but her sense of humour is beaten by

the dread of having yet another mess
labelled and placed out of reach.
She remembers a dress that her parents liked
and decides that from now on she'll wear it.

Her sister no longer trusts herself;
the room has become a hall of mirrors
and she cannot detect any true image,
or the reflection that she is used to.

The youngest has closed his eyes.
He keeps seeing a car crash that he
witnessed but never discussed:
how a door opened and a body fell out.

Maggie Hannan

COMING DOWN FROM DERRY HILL

During my sister's birth
you were at the cinema
watching Bardot, I think,
or was it Monroe?
Ploughing your blond hair
with a huge hand and packing
tobacco in a pipe.

You kept mink then
and fed them on tripe –
it stank,
mingling with the sweet
stench of litter and
dank musk of mink.
I clung onto you –

Baggy-trousered Dad,
my hand fisted in yours,
tip-toeing slyly past rows
of pinch-faced creatures
curled in whorls against wire
like furred snails.
You gave them no names.

I saw you leave the shed
swinging a brace of mink
doll-bodied and loose
like cats in ample skins,
and a door shuttering

to and fro; a whiff of gas
sloughed off in the breeze.

Coming down from Derry Hill
to our cottage, you'd enter
gladly, sprawl yourself,
all legs and fingers
tapping to the Beatles
or jazz, and wink at me once
from the black chair.

HIGH HOLCOMBE

Turn again – see
it all spread out,
the land slip down
to toe the ocean,

night beginning
with fluorescent blaze
along the quay,
illumination

of a child's tracks
crabbing the sand.
From up here, it
all seems small –

only the foot's
tension on the slope,
just the weight of
walking – feel

the body's charge
meet the task
yard by yard, hear
the quickening

pulse of tides below;
for a moment, briefly,
inhabit the bird
ascending.

THE BONE DIE

Even the wrist's fast jack
is funked by a thumb's rub,

chances and freaked odds
of plane, pit, dot and dot

are pocketed or scuttled.
A weathered die contrives

its craft of luck over years –
edges all unwhet, or honed

in captivities of palm. Thrown
down for a free run (an ack ack

clatter after gulling), its pulling
up dead on a rising surface,

jinxes still by a worn slant.
Two up, two up, where fractures web

the sockets of its eyes – askance –
laugh lines – a probability of chaos.

TOM PASSEY'S CHILD

Unremarkable at first, this infant,
bedded down and silent in a cot,
fingers shoaling at the blanket's edge –
'Hold him' – I hesitate, cautious
of what might be discovered, then
some instinct draws my hand to his.

The grip's not right, tensile –
he begins the search for focus
and fails, staring up as if through
depths of water –
I reach down for him:
the shock of his weightlessness,

the dreadful stillness of his gaze!
Held close, his breathing's fierce
and sharp against my cheek,
the effort precocious. Like this
Tom Passey finds us, transfixed,
all things fallen quiet at his exposure.

Tom's deliberate clatter at the sink,
his leaving for the garden – the words
'His sickness sickens me also.'
Outside he is quickly busy,
a thumbprint marking every seedling
bedded down and silent in the ground.

William Park

NATURAL ALIENS

We couldn't relate, Hydrozoa.
You had a combined mouth
and anus;
your companion
had batteries of stinging cells.
Yours was a freakish environment.
Sometimes, at night
I caught my reflection
in the dark mirror,
wondered
if I could secrete my skeleton also.
Dreams were filled
with jelly umbrellas;
bells, like muscles
pulsated through black waters.
Some of you
still float by, like irises,
across the ink inside my mind.

Me, and a cabin,
and the sea.
It was unnatural.
I needed you.
Not the Medusae –
sea wasps, nor the fire jellies
could calm my disturbance.
There were killer X-rays moving
against the black film of the ocean.
An arrangement of lips

hoarded their death-sting.
I needed your voice.
Not the threat
of gelatinous blades
or the subtle hanging
of Oriental curtains.
From those transparencies
anything could invisibly strike.

The Anthozoa were more solid:
soft corals,
brick red.
Others were organ-pipe skeletons
or new homes for sponges.
Later, my eyes glittered
over their slides.
For a moment
your ghost on the wall
stopped me:
I thought you were here.
Then, anemones
vied for my love
with sticky tentacles.
Coral was like coloured bone.
When it died
its bleached white skeleton
lay behind like a fossil.

I left in the wake of Crustaceans,
spider crabs, armour-plated.
They had a defence, but I
in a position of strength
was weaker.
I sensed I was alien.
Some were sheathed

by transparency, their cast-off skins
perfect replicas.
They had compound eyes.
Some changed colour
when they ate.
That night, in the cabin's bathroom
my dead skin turned white.
The blades of my penknife
shut
like the claws
of the mantis shrimp.

THE FISHERMEN

Out here, there's meditation,
black boots and green umbrellas.
I have to step over rods
to make sure I don't kick them,
and pass squat figures on seats
with their backs against the sun.
They're watching for 'miller's thumb'.

What's brought them here is water.
It's an inferior kind,
and I can't help but puzzle
about their motivations
for sitting in cold weather
with the clouds hiding the sun.
Watching the rain can't be fun.

But a man smoking his pipe
greets me with tranquillity,
while the others are busy
being still, thinking, waiting.
There must be something for them:
if not fish, a place to share
their skill with lines, and canned beer.

Late at night, the river runs
like a black arm on my right.
The fishermen have gone home,
and I'm walking back to yours.
Fish swim. I philosophize:
if fish aren't figments we share,
they must be real, and out there.

THE WANTED CHILD

Come here. Don't leave
before you've arrived.
You're wanted. I've painted
one whole room blue for you.
If that's your colour. Right now
you're shapeless, I can't hear you
except how you steal
into my words, taking root,
sustenance.
Soon I'll be ill because of you,
soon I'll be complete.

Don't expect favours:
this is no heaven.
The house is clean,
the garden's tended.
Things have begun to bloom.
Not once have I ravaged
the ground of roses,
but forked my anger inward.
So you'll find me thin –
less to cuddle,
less to hurt.

You'll notice
the garden will change:
snow will fall,
rain fall, leaves fall.
The truth is,
you'll grow old, weaken,
and I won't be here.

Don Paterson

THE ROUND-TRIP

The train flirts with the coast, then heads inland.
Through gaps between factories, shuttling powerlines,
man-made thunderheads, rupturing ozone
the sun is going down again, thinking of England

but remodelling, with its tactile memory,
the ancient and private geographies –
continents of scoria, condensing seas;
the kind of lurid, ritual mummery

we're all suckers for. It makes him look a dunce –
the involuntary rush of *schwärmerei*
turns him crimson, while he faces out the sky
quite lost, until the dull fact slowly dawns:

habit is only death on the move.
Tonight, alone, he will replay to himself
those other girls in silent lap dissolve
while he makes love to the woman he does not love.

SHHH

Then, it was natural to hear the sea
cautiously remembered
in those calcified air-locks and chambers
though I knew it might as well be
anything – forest fires, landslides, hurricanes
falsified by distance
or amplification; the white noise
of the wilder elements

or the wash of chaos
as she puts her lips to your ear
and through canal and cochlea you catch
the general drift – the old blandishments,
the sweet nothings, the breath drawn at your touch:
I no longer believe what I hear.

CONSPIRACIES

Crouched behind the sideboard with my mother
I heard the travelling salesman at the door;
'We're oot. Last thing yer faither needs 's another
shavin'-brush.' Crawling along the floor
we edged the curtain back and had a snigger
as he lugged his battered trunk back down the street.
Two or three years later, when I was bigger,
returning with the groceries, she'd meet
me at the door with 'Sorry! No' the day . . .'
I'd wedge my foot to keep the door ajar
till finally she'd weaken and give way,
though I'd worry that she'd take the game too far.

See how the second blade shaves closer still:
last night, in our break-up's silent aftermath,
I felt as though I had returned, the prodigal –
dragging my cardboard suitcase up the path,
relieved to witness how the perfect front
still conducts home's gentle innuendo;
the mutter of known voices, the hearth's mild taunt,
a patch of breath still shrinking on the window
as the lights wink out and something stirs behind
the curtain; double-checking the nameplate
I fumble with old keys, only to find
the locks changed; you're pretending to be out.

PERIGEE

Freak alignments. I am the best man,
she, the bridesmaid. John, the resident MC
once our playground quarry, does not complain
when we corner him, frisking for his master key.

Our affair was stripped of all the usual padding –
just a flat joke about not getting committed
and a serviceable number by Joan Armatrading –
but we honed the *ruses de guerre* that first outwitted,
then destroyed our partners. I'd do sentry duty,
she, the dangerous stuff – who wouldn't trust her?

Posted at the door, I watch her spike
the marriage bed with handfuls of confetti,
discreet as fallout. Smiling, she swings back
towards me again, a natural disaster.

RESTITUTION

The Book of Change, through all my feverish dealings
produced the same response: 'Li. Flaming Beauty.'
Her note came late, as if, to spare my feelings
the postman had snuck round with it, off-duty.
I threw the coins and watched them chatter down
then turned up the inevitable gloss;
'so great is the obstruction that the sun
appears as a tiny star.'

I've kept her letters, still cheap-scented, vital,
pressing the life from them between my books;
shook out the straws of sentimental detail,
placed half aside, discarding the remainder.
Cropped to a line's length, they lie in stooks
as trim as yarrow stalks, as dry as tinder.

John Wells

SAM WILD'S HOUSE

Now his home bears his name:
the privet grown out of line,
spreading above the pavement
from a rank of trim hedges;
the grass, holed up in tussocks,
littered with scrap wood and
sheared polystyrene blocks;
the path's asphalt pulled out
leaving a leafmulch strip
tracking to splintered chipboard
fixed across the doorway;
the upstairs windows shuttered
with oblong hunks of perspex
bolted over their frames,
the downstairs window grilled,
and central, a circular
blue plaque on the brick red:
Sam Wild, Commander of the
British Battalion of the
International Brigade
in the Spanish Civil War,
lived here, for nineteen years.
I hadn't heard of him,
but I can conjecture
his front room lit past midnight
as he went at new concerns,
someone striding through Birchfields
past the football players,
bitter at Spain for the work

put in for no return; now
his effort's absence marked
by his home's dereliction
in the dim street. Next door
the net curtains are parted
on jugs of late flowers,
and the woodwork's gloss green.
Lived in, it is kept up,
old seedheads cleared from the sills,
paint lids tight in the shed;
like Spain, aired and refurbished.

SCIANT OMNES

The parchment is a roll-call,
a row of survivors.
The rest of the vill are waste,
lime on a fallow field
that has stiffened to plain rock.

So we keep the company of
sinners: Mathew atte Slade
brewed bad ale, his
daughter Agnes sold it. Know
all men, they were fined pennies.

I split the Latin sediment
to find these imprints of fossil,
flecks of dried movement
still working on the manor
rolls in a closed archive.

COLLEGE LIBRARY

Every brain is soaked
in a different dye: Hegel,
tapeworms, pistons or sonatas;

but a girl skins a bright orange,
and sends the smell of her fruit
into all our heads.

HOUSE AND HOME

Houses, he thinks, are like women,
although much easier to love:
always one imperfection or other
aches on his contentment – a curl
of wallpaper, a tap dripping;
'But we must live with them.'
You are stuck in Clarendon's throat
and Macaulay's spine is intact.
Your mother calls from the kitchen
for hours; her words stick on the walls
like pollen. Quietly your father
pushes the door to. Pawing at Gibbons,
he tweezers the stamps into place.

We walk the length of the garden
from the back porch, stretching out
behind the tent of runner beans.
The tangle and nonsense of weeds
is not a ruin: the plot grows
headlong, its essences unstoppered.
Here at last we talk, kiss,
conspire in the green light.
Soon one of your parents will
check us; they never carry hoes or
trowels for excuses. Each evening
over dinner your father talks of
selling us this land for our home.

LITTLE MEN

A college friend
describes the little men
his family has:

one with no hair
at all for lights
and wiring,

another for when
the oven won't heat up,
another for the times

you come back home
and find the kitchen's
full of water . . .

he admires them
for their speed
and cleanliness.

Wellses
had always been
little men –

we'd come and clear
the skirting board
of dry rot,

or provide
a better handrail
for the stairs.

Biographical Notes

STEVE ANTHONY was born in London in 1958 and educated at the Universities of Hull and Stirling, where he took an M.Phil. in Modern Poetry. He works as a lecturer in Further Education. His poems have appeared in various magazines and have won prizes in a number of competitions, including the Bloodaxe Poetry Book Competition in 1987.

MAURA DOOLEY was born and raised in the West Country. She studied at York and Bristol Universities. She now lives and works in London. Her published works include *Ivy Leaves and Arrows* (Bloodaxe, 1987), *Turbulence* (Giant Steps Press, 1988) and *Singing Brink* (ed with David Hunter; Arvon Press, 1987. A new collection is due from Bloodaxe in November 1990.

STEPHEN KNIGHT was born in Swansea in 1960. He read English at Oxford. His poems have appeared in many magazines and anthologies, including *London Magazine*, *New Statesman & Society*, *The Times Literary Supplement* and *Poetry Introduction 6* (Faber, 1985). He has worked as a writer-in-residence for West Glamorgan and as a theatre director in Leatherhead, Swansea and on the London Fringe.

PETER MCDONALD was born in Belfast in 1965. He read English at Oxford and was elected Research Lecturer at Christ Church, Oxford in 1986. His publications include *Trio Poetry 3* (Blackstaff Press) and *New Chatto Poets*. He won the Newdigate Prize in 1983.

JILL MAUGHAN was born in 1958 in Newcastle and educated in Darlington. After working in journalism and social work, she took a degree in Communication Studies at Sunderland Polytechnic and then worked as a Publicity Officer at Cashe Chase Community Arts Centre in Durham City. She is currently writing her second children's novel and completing a full collection of poems. Her publications include *Ghosts at Four O'Clock* (Bloodaxe) and *The Deceivers* (Collins Armada).

PAUL MUNDEN was born in 1958 in Poole, Dorset. He was educated at the University of York, where he has since run an extended series of writing workshops. He formed the Jazz & Poetry Group 'Tortoise' and was awarded a Writer's Bursary by Yorkshire Arts Association in 1982. He has won prizes in the Kent Literature Festival and the Yorkshire Open Poetry Competition. Since receiving a Gregory Award in 1987, he has worked as a freelance writer, also editing novels for film. A selection of his work appears in Faber's *Poetry Introduction 7*. He lives near Castle Howard, York, which formed the subject of a sequence of poems, 'Henderskelfe', exhibited with accompanying photographs at the Castle in 1989. He is married, with two daughters.

SIMON ARMITAGE was born in 1963, and lives in Huddersfield. His first full-length collection, *Zoom!*, was published by Bloodaxe Books in 1989, and is a Poetry Book Society Choice.

ADRIAN BLACKLEDGE is 30 years old. He lives with his wife and three children in Birmingham, and is a primary school teacher. His poems have been published in various journals including the *Spectator*, *Encounter*, *London Magazine* and *Orbis*.

ROBERT CRAWFORD was born at Bellshill near Glasgow in 1959. He grew up in Glasgow. After graduating in English from Glasgow University, he spent six years pursuing research at Oxford, then returned to Scotland where he is now a Lecturer in Modern Scottish Literature in the Department of English at the University of St Andrews. He is an editor of the international magazine *Verse*. His collections of poems include *A Scottish Assembly* (Chatto, 1990) and the book of Scots verse *Sharawaggi*, shared with W.N. Herbert (Polygon, 1990). He has written and edited books on T.S. Eliot and Edwin Morgan.

GWYNETH LEWIS was born in Cardiff in 1959 and is bilingual in Welsh and English. She went to Cambridge to study English, and then to America as a Harkness Fellow, where she studied at Harvard, and at the Graduate Writing Division in Columbia. She worked in New York as a freelance journalist before going to Oxford to write a doctoral thesis on literary forgeries. She now works as a television journalist in Cardiff. Her poems have appeared in the *TLS*, the *New Statesman*, *NER/Breadloaf Quarterly*, *Verse* and *Poetry Review*. Her first book of Welsh poetry, *Soneday Redsa*, was published by Gomer Press in 1990.

MICHAEL SYMMONS ROBERTS was born in 1963 in Preston, Lancashire. He read Philosophy and Theology at Oxford, and now lives in Cardiff where he works as a BBC Radio Producer. His poems have been published in *London Magazine*, *The Times Literary Supplement*, *Ambit*, *Verse*, *Poetry Wales* and *Blank Page*; and broadcast on Kaleidoscope (Radio 4), World Service, LBC Radio and TVS. 'The Allotment' was a prizewinner in the 1985 Cheltenham Festival Competition.

PAUL HENRY was born in Aberystwyth, and grew up there and in two Breconshire villages, Llangynidr and Llangorse. He studied English Literature and Theatre Arts at Rolle College, Exmouth. He originally wrote songs in Welsh and English, which were broadcast on national radio and television. His poems have appeared in various journals. He currently lives in Gwent.

DAVID MORLEY was born in Lancashire in 1964. He read Zoology at Bristol University, and received a Ph.D. at London University. He researched acid rain in Cumbria. He is currently a freelance poet, a writing tutor, editor, and Director of *Poetry Network*. During the 1989 revolutions he was a Berlin and Prague correspondent for United Newspapers and several magazines. He has had poems broadcast on BBC World Service, BBC Radio Cumbria, Tyne Tees TV, BBC North East and BBC Radio Lancashire.

KATRINA PORTEOUS was born in Aberdeen in 1960 and moved to Consett, Co. Durham in 1967. She graduated from Trinity Hall, Cambridge in 1982, and during 1982–84 she lived in the United States, writing and studying poetry at Berkeley and Harvard Universities. She now lives and works as a freelance writer in North Northumberland.

Her poems have appeared in several anthologies, including *Trees be Company*, ed Angela King and Sue Clifford for Common Ground; and a forthcoming Anthology from Bloodaxe Books, entitled *Eve Sharing – new women poets*, edited by Fleur Adcock. Various of her short stories and articles have been published in popular magazines and national newspapers including *Woman* and *The Guardian*. She has also written *Beadneall: A history in Photographs*, to be published by Northumberland County Council in 1990.

138

GERARD WOODWARD was born in London in 1961, and educated at Falmouth School of Art and the London School of Economics. He has had poetry published in many magazines, including the *Spectator*, the *TLS*, *Ambit*, *Encounter*, *Poetry Review* and *Stand*. He has published *The Unwriter and Other Poems* (Sycamore Press 1989) and is included in the forthcoming anthology *Anvil New Voices*. Chatto and Windus will publish a full collection in 1991.

JONATHAN DAVIDSON was born in Oxfordshire in 1964. He took a degree in Performing Arts (majoring in Arts Administration) from Leicester Polytechnic. He currently lives in Scunthorpe and is a Literature Development Worker from South Humberside.

NICHOLAS DRAKE was born in 1961. His family are from Prague. His published work includes a study of Yeats (Penguin 1990), contributions to the *Cambridge Guide to Literature and English*, and poems in several magazines. He won a Duncan Lawrie prize in the *Observer*/Arvon Foundation Competition in 1989. A pamphlet, *The Disappearing City*, is published by Mandeville Press (1990).

LAVINIA GREENLAW was born in 1962. She grew up in Essex and London where she now lives. She works as an editor.

MAGGIE HANNAN was born in 1962 in Wiltshire, and lived in Derbyshire and Sheffield before moving to Cumbria. She has worked as a monumental mason and life model, and is currently unemployed. She received the Tyrone Guthrie Award from Northern Arts in 1988, and has contributed to *New Lake Poets* ed William Scammell (Bloodaxe), due to be published in 1990.

WILLIAM PARK was born in 1962 in West London. He currently lives in Preston, Lancashire. Amongst other jobs, he was a psychiatric nurse for 3 years, and is now a Creative Writing tutor. In the summer of 1989 he was Writer in Residence at St Martin's College, Lancaster. His first novel was recently shortlisted for the Constable Trophy, and his poems are appearing in numerous magazines and anthologies, including: *Ambit*, *Outposts*, *Acumen*, *The Green Book*, *Poetry Durham*, *Iron*, *The Rialto*.

DON PATERSON was born in Dundee in 1963. He is a musician and has performed in Jazz festivals in Europe. He now lives in Brighton.

JOHN WELLS was born in 1964 in Newbury, Berkshire, and educated at St. Bartholomew's School, Newbury. He read History at Trinity Hall, Cambridge. He is currently working as the researcher for a project based in the University of Reading Library. In 1987 a pamphlet collection, *Ambion Hill*, was published by the Mandeville Press.

Acknowledgements List

STEVE ANTHONY

'Trading Tools' has appeared in 'Orbis'.
'Earthswimmer' has appeared in *Sound Press for the Blind*.
'Her Final Performance' was awarded second prize in the
  Civil Service National Poetry Competition 1987 and
  published in the civil service writers' magazine, 'The
  Author'.

STEPHEN KNIGHT

'The Awkward Age': a prizewinner 1984 National Poetry
  Comp./Poetry Introduction, 6.
'In Case of Monsters': Argo (forthcoming).
'The Gift': *London Review of Books*/*Poetry Introduction 6*
  (Faber, 1985)/Against the Grain (Nelson, 1989).
'SHC' Poetry Now (BBC Radio 3)/*The Times Literary
  Supplement*.

JILL MAUGHAN

'Hill End', 'Vase', 'Ghost of Love', 'Two Doors Up' have all
  appeared in *Ghosts at Four O'clock* (Bloodaxe Books 1986)
  as well as in the Bloodaxe anthology *Four Pack no.1, Four
  From Northern Women*.

PAUL MUNDEN

'The Practice Room' was broadcast on *Poetry Now* (BBC
  Radio 3) and published in *Poetry Introduction 7* (Faber &
  Faber).
'Dance' published in *She* magazine.
'Tie-ins' published in *New Statesman & Society*.
'Sold' published in *The New Writer*.
'Ten Years On' won a prize in the Yorkshire Open Poetry
  Competition 1989.

SIMON ARMITAGE

'Greenhouse' – *London Magazine*, Slow Dancer Press,
  Bloodaxe Books.
'Very Simply Topping Up The Brake Fluid' – *Iron* Magazine,
  The Wide Skirt Press, Bloodaxe Books.
'Why Write of the Sun' – Giant Steps, Slow Dancer Press,
  Bloodaxe Books.
'This Time Last Year' – Slow Dancer Press, Bloodaxe Books.

ADRIAN BLACKLEDGE

'Woken at Two' appeared in *Orbis* Magazine.

ROBERT CRAWFORD – All poems are reproduced from
  Robert Crawford, *A Scottish Assembly* (Chatto 1990).

GWYNETH LEWIS – 'The Bad Shepherd' has appeared in
  Verse.

MICHAEL SYMMONS ROBERTS

'The Allotment' was a prizewinner in the 1985 Cheltenham
  Festival Poetry Competition, and was published in *The
  Times Literary Supplement*.

PAUL HENRY

'Retired' – first appeared in *Poetry Wales*.
'Widows of Talyllyn' – an earlier version was published in
  South West Review.
'Cwm Dyffryn' – due to appear in *New Welsh Review*.

DAVID MORLEY

BBC Radio Cumbria, BBC World Service, *London Magazine*, *Poems of the Scottish Hills* (AUP, 1983), *Poetry Introduction 7* (Faber & Faber, 1990), *Releasing Stone* (Littlewood Press, 1989), *Rialto*, *Staple*, *The University Supplement*.

KATRINA PORTEOUS

'If My Train Will Come' – Highly commended in Lincoln Age Concern Open Poetry Competition 1987.
'Gone Again' – Arvon Course Prizewinner in Newcastle Evening Chronicle Poetry Competition 1988 – appeared in Newcastle Evening Chronicle December 30 1988.

GERARD WOODWARD

'Suffolk Interior' appeared in the booklet *The Unwriter & Other Poems* (Sycamore Press) and also won a prize in 1987 National Poetry Competition and was broadcast on BBC Radio 3 and Radio Manchester.
'Maiden Voyage' has been accepted by Poetry Nottingham.

JONATHAN DAVIDSON – 'The Trainspotter' in *Poetry and Audience*.

NICHOLAS DRAKE – 'The Disappearing City' published by Mandeville Press (1990).

LAVINIA GREENLAW

'North' first appeared in *Stand*.
'A Change in the Weather' and 'Resistance' first appeared in *The Wide Skirt*.

MAGGIE HANNAN

'Coming Down From Derry Hill' – Staple, BBC Radio
Cumbria, Bloodaxe Books*.
'Tom Passey's Child' – Bloodaxe Books*.
'The Bone Die' – Bloodaxe Books*.

*Publication due Summer 1990

JOHN WELLS

'Sciant Omnes', 'College Library' and 'Little Men' were
published in his pamphlet collection *Ambion Hill* (The
Mandeville Press, 1987); of these, 'Sciant Omnes' was first
published in *Virtue Without Terror*.
'House and Home' was published in The Newbury Arts
Workshop Poetry Group Competition Anthology, 1985.